SOMEHOW
I THOUGHT I WOULD
BE TALLER

Finding the Courage You Need to Grow

Personally

Professionally

~~**Physically**~~

JEFF VANEK

JD, MST, and a little BS

Somehow, I Thought I Would Be Taller –
Finding the Courage You Need To Grow Personally & Professionally.

By Jeff Vanek

Book Categories: Humor, Career, Self-Help

Book cover design and layout by Kristy Witt

Published by Scruffy Dog, LLC

First Edition, May 2015

ISBN 978-0-9861412-0-1

This book is dedicated to you, *the reader.*

May you find the courage you need to grow.

As E.E. Cummings penned, *"It takes courage to grow up and become who you really are."* I believe you will find that courage. Count me in as one of your cheerleaders in your journey to be a taller you.

Jeff Vanek

Contents

The Tall and Short of Things

Being tall isn't a matter of feet or inches.
It's a matter of courage.

I grew up short. That had not been my plan. I am a good four inches–okay, four and a half inches–shorter than the average American male. My physical stature is one thing but what really got to me was how I came up short in life when it came to my big expectations of success. I, like you, had big dreams and high hopes. Things didn't necessarily turn out like I thought they would.

I spent years reading self-help literature, which gave me my grand ideas about life and who I would be. I started reading books like *Think and Grow Rich* and *As a Man Thinketh* in my teen years, moving on to *The Seven Habits of Highly Effective People* and its ilk as time went on. I read Blanchard, Canfield, Carnegie, Covey, Dyer, Emerson, Frankl, Franklin, and on down the alphabet of literary luminaries of self-help. I learned all about positive mental attitudes, habits of success, time management, effective speaking, getting rich, staying healthy, awakening the giant within, and being younger next year. Self-help literature had been my drug of choice. I wanted to think and get rich, live big, come to

understand that I was actually from Mars and not Earth when it came to relationships, and be younger with each passing year.

In spite of the buzz I felt as I finished off another self-help book or listened to another motivational speaker, I am not sure how much it changed what I actually did. Oh, I would be motivated in the moment, ready to change my life and the world. That feeling would last a few hours at best and ultimately I would change nothing. Like a night of passion with a lover, there would be anticipation and excitement. At least with a night of passion there might be a new life created. I had no such luck, however, with the motivational stuff.

I dreamed of open, honest, deep, and meaningful relationships–with a scorching hot love life. I imagined never putting on extra pounds, at least not pounds of fat. It was going to be all well-toned, solid muscle. I would drive an expensive imported sports car–which I would park in the garage of my dream home.

All those expectations about how my life was going to be never worked out. My relationships were for the most part shallow and superficial. As for the car I drove–think "nondescript and practical". And no, I don't park my nondescript and practical car in the garage of my dream home. As for my love life, it is personal and none of your business. And as for my weight, let's just leave it at: I wasn't getting heavier from well-built muscle. In short, somehow I thought I would be taller.

I read motivational how-to books. I made lists. I wrote goals. I repeated mantras. I taped up motivational quotes on my bedroom walls and in my office at work. I patted my head and rubbed my tummy at the same time. Maybe I just hadn't tried hard enough. Maybe I needed to be patting my head and rubbing my tummy while walking and chewing gum. There was always something more I should be doing, or doing differently, or not doing, or thinking about or not thinking about, or changing or not changing–always something more depending on who I listened to or read. I was just never good enough and my field of dreams remained an empty field full of weeds of disappointment. I wondered why. I was tired of sitting in the bleachers of life looking at my weed-choked field of dreams.

I was done physically growing, at least in height–and I wasn't interested in growing in girth. My youngest son had a suggestion for me when he heard I wanted to be taller. He pulled out a kitchen chair and told to me to stand on it, "This will make you taller," he said. He had a good idea–find what you need to make you taller.

What I wanted to do was to grow personally, professionally, intellectually, and financially. Why is it that so many people find themselves in life wondering why things didn't turn out like they had hoped they would? Things will go wrong. How will you make them right? What "chair" do you need to stand on to be taller?

I have come to believe that the reason most of us fail to achieve our dreams isn't lack of opportunity, talent, ability, skill, or intellect. It's an abundance of fear. I lacked courage. I knew I did. Not to be petty and jealous–which I certainly can be–but I have seen it time and time again. Untalented idiots who, in spite of their lack of talent or intelligence, are nevertheless courageous in how they live their lives–and they achieve amazing things. I wanted to be courageous. I knew I had to be courageous if I wanted to see a difference in my own life. Even if I wasn't the sharpest tack in the box at least I recognized that it was fear that was holding me back.

Call me an optimist, maybe a foolish one, but I still had hope. I wasn't ready to call it quits on my dreams. I didn't want to give up. I wanted to believe I could still change, still grow. So I contemplated my bellybutton, looked deeply into my soul, and decided to take a closer look at the man in the mirror–bad mistake. I no longer had hair on my head–it seemed to have migrated to other parts of my body. Putting looks aside, I realized something important. If I was going to pursue my dreams in earnest, I was going to need courage.

I have seen what courage can do for a person. It can make up for a lack of talent, skill, ability, experience, physical or mental resources, and opportunity. Even so, neither you nor I are totally bereft of these various attributes. True, you have more of some, less of others. Even so, you may find you have more than you thought you had if you take a moment to think about it. Sometimes it takes looking at yourself and life in a new way to see what has always been there.

So what does it mean to have courage? I was committed to finding out–not institutional type of committed–but dedicated to finding out what courage is. (Not that being a little crazy at times won't hurt.) So what do you have to do to find courage? Walk on fire barefoot? Does that give you courage? In short, yes–if you want to be a professional stuntman. For those of us who have other ideas about careers and life aspirations, however, finding the courage needed to grow will mean taking a different path. Not an easier path, necessarily. Like I found, walking over fire barefoot is easy compared to what it often takes for you to have the courage to grow. Even so, courage is not just for the brave, the talented, the gifted or lucky idiots, it is for you if you want it enough. Courage is a mindset. Big expectations take thinking taller and courage comes when you think taller. In short, you can always think taller.

What does it mean to think taller? That depends on you. What follows are the things I found helpful in my attempt to think taller in my own life. I am confident you will find them equally helpful. No matter how short you may have come up in life, you must think taller if you want to have the courage you need to achieve those un-fulfilled dreams of yours.

✷ EXPERIENCE A GROWTH SPURT ✷

To be taller, start thinking taller.

Coming Out of the Right Closet

*It takes a lot of energy to be someone you aren't,
nor are you ever really good at it.*

Who are you? Not who you pretend to be. Not who you think you should or need to be. But who are you really? This can be a disturbing question. It is, however, an important question that needs to be answered honestly. Reality may bite, but it must be dealt with if you expect to grow.

For me, it meant coming to terms with the fact that I was a right brain thinker in a left brain dominated world. So I faked left brain orientation. I pretended to be something, someone I wasn't, fearing I would be viewed as irresponsible and a flake for wanting to pursue more creative paths in life. After all, who in their right mind wants to be a flake or be thought of as one? True, there are people who are irresponsible, but it isn't something most—even those that are irresponsible—aspire to be. When it came to planning my career, I did not want to be a flake. To my way of thinking, people who involved themselves in areas smacking of right brain use were kind of flakey—artists, actors, writers, dancers, painters, illustrators, flower

arrangers, but not wedding planners. Wedding planners need a lot of left brain power–they have to be good with logistics.

Most people like the idea of creativity and creative careers. Most people do not ultimately want to go into them. In a *Slate* article, *"Inside The Box–People Don't Actually Like Creativity,"* by Jessica Oliea, she writes "People are biased against creative thinking, despite all of their insistence otherwise." She then quotes Barry Staw, a Professor at the Haas School of Business, University of California, Berkeley, who specializes in creativity, "We think of creative people in a heroic manner, and we celebrate them, but the thing we celebrate is the after-effect."

We like to see creative things but we don't really like the creative process, especially in business where real money is involved. The creative process is often messy, wasteful, full of trial and errors, missteps, and going back to the "drawing board." There is a lot of failure involved in the creative process in time, effort, and money. Most people (and companies) would rather do without all of that and just skip to the success part of creativity–the end result that actually works.

I had always considered most creative fields to be high risk endeavors in terms of financial reward, and therefore a flakey path to pursue. Not that financial reward is everything. I just didn't think starving artist was a very cool route to go. I thought the business world would be my best bet. Successful professionals are respected, honored, and generally thought of as icons of our capitalist society. I quickly realized, however, that I wasn't really into business kinds of things or classes as I went through college. I was more into communications, ideas, concepts, and as much as I denied it, I really found all those right brain oriented subjects quite interesting–very interesting–which alarmed me. I liked my acting and communication classes but could not bring myself to think of them as career worthy. I needed to find a "real" career.

I, like many, thought education and choosing the right work would ensure that I achieved a degree of both professional and personal success in life. I was going to achieve the life promised by every multilevel marketing company for hawking their health supplements, household products, and miracle juices–except I was going to build my success on the backs of strangers, not friends and family who I recruited to be in my down-line. I decided to take the ethical route and be a corporate attorney.

So I went to law school to find fame and fortune. I figured law school was a kind of cheater's path into business for someone like me. It was a way to be involved in the business world without having to study things like accounting, finance, management and economics. Sure, you have to know a little something about those fields, but you don't have to study them in law school. I was quite content to let the business, accounting, and economic majors study those subjects. Corporate law sounded about right to me, as well as prestigious and lucrative. I just ignored the fact that good corporate lawyers really do need a good understanding of what makes corporations run–all that accounting and finance stuff.

I found the language and tools of business–numbers and spreadsheets–boring, sometimes confusing, and foreign to my way of thinking about the world. I understood that numbers are useful–for something. I just had a hard time finding what that something was. To this day I don't remember most phone numbers. I don't know my times tables either–really–no joke. It's not that I haven't tried to memorize them–first in grade school and then again before I started my master's program. Neither time worked–I am still totally dependent on fingers and calculators.

Sure, I like big numbers–when they are in my bank account–which unfortunately has remained theoretical speculation on my part. I would like to test that theory someday. I am sure big numbers in my bank account would be enjoyable. My reality is that I am much more in love with ideas and concepts. I am much more comfortable, and have no problem with confronting abstract and fuzzy concepts. I am energized writing a sentence as opposed to creating a formula on a spreadsheet. Give me a bunch of ideas and I will find a connection and a story in them.

One of the problems with trying to be someone you're not is that people assume things about you that aren't true. They have expectations in their minds about skills or traits you have. This happens to me all the time as an attorney. For example, people often think I am a detail-oriented person because I am an attorney. I have no idea where they get that notion about attorneys–from contract reading and drafting maybe? So I would often pretend that I was detailed and numerically oriented, and even do my best to be so, but in fact, I was not.

While on the subject of personal deficiencies, don't ask me for directions, if you want to actually get to your destination. I often confuse my right and left. One year when I was in high school, for Christmas my parents actually gave me gloves with right and left printed on them as a joke–sort of. Maybe the right and left confusion is dyslexia? My wife is convinced it is. Rather than elaborate on the traits often manifested by dyslexics, let's just say that spellcheck doesn't always know what I am trying to write. My spelling isn't always what you would call "Standard English." Thankfully, autofill on the web browser comes to my rescue when spellcheck has failed me, especially when the search results come back with, "Did you mean: ____?" "Yes, that was exactly what I meant," I often find myself thinking. At least some algorithm understands what I am trying to write.

I have been very inspired by the quote from James Wooden, "Do not let what you cannot do interfere with what you can do." I have never let my inability to spell stop me from writing. I found a great deal of pleasure in writing and just kept doing more of it–spellcheck failures and all. Even when writing business articles, there is a creative process of ideas and storytelling that is energizing.

I tried to find a good compromise between my real interests and the corporate world where I felt the "good jobs" were. To that end, an opportunity to go into human resources came my way. I figured the more I could work with people, the better off I would be. I found working with people a good thing–most of the time. It was in a big organization that provided me with a regular paycheck, good health insurance, an expense account for travel, 401(k) with employer match, and a pension, not to mention the other employee perks like free sixth row center court tickets to the local NBA games. This all seemed like a pretty good gig.

The problem was that I still wasn't really being who I was or doing what I loved. I was making a living but not really living. I found myself miserable and feeling like I was dying inside. This was a good job in a good company with good co-workers. Even so, by trying to be what I wasn't or rather feeling like I had to hide who I was, the results were tension headaches almost every day and eating Excedrin Extra Strength tablets like they were candy. I didn't even use water to chase down the Excedrin. I just chewed them up and swallowed. Sure they were bitter but so was my internal conflict. It felt like my soul was being sucked from me each day I woke up and went into the office. Yet I soldiered on and ate my Excedrin, yum, yum.

Why rock the boat and come out of your closet? Why be who you really are and stop hiding it from others–or from yourself? Does it really matter what you hide? Why not just keep pretending if it's working? Because ultimately it doesn't work–nor is it sustainable. No matter how good you may be at hiding your true self, there are consequences–and they are not good consequences.

In a study conducted by Dr. Clayton R. Critcher from the University of California, Berkeley, and Dr. Melissa J. Ferguson from Cornell University, participants were asked to conceal information about themselves. Several tests were conducted to determine the effects that concealing information had on a person. In each case, test participants showed measurable and significant depletion in their cognitive, interpersonal, and even in their physical abilities. Interestingly, all test participants were heterosexual but they were asked to hide a homosexual orientation for the purposes of the test. The very act of having to hide information about yourself, even if wasn't true, was enough to impair a person's abilities in the three areas tested. It was also true even when participants were asked not to reveal neutral information that had nothing to do with sexual orientation.

What if that information about yourself is true. What if that information has social stigmas or your own personal stigmas attached to it? The study showed that when you conceal information, that alone takes a toll on you. Other studies have shown that if that information has a stigma attached to it (put there by society or yourself), it also takes a significant toll on mental and physical health. As Critcher and Ferguson pointed out in their study, hiding your identity is exhausting.

When we conceal core information about ourselves, it affects our ability to perform our job—or to be a human being. It affects us emotionally, which in turn has an effect on those we interact with—co-workers, bosses, family, friends, the clerk at the grocery checkout. If you have been someone who has concealed your true self, the "real you," you already know what it does to you and your emotional, intellectual, and physical self. You know the price you pay. It takes a lot of energy being someone you aren't or as the study showed, hiding information about yourself. So why do you do it?

There are a lot of reasons—you don't like who you are; you are afraid to let others see the real you for fear of what they will think; you believe that the façade you put up is necessary to maintain your job, relationships, and lifestyle; you are scared of what others, whose opinions you value (parents, spouse, friends, supervisor, boss) will think. Let's be honest. What others think about you will change if you reveal your true self when you have been working so hard to be someone else. What you think about yourself will also change. Are those necessarily bad things? No. Often they are better things—even the best things. But it does take courage to be you, the real you.

Things unraveled for me at my "great corporate job" when a merger took place. With the merger came a reassignment of my responsibilities. My position as Director of Human Resources became a redundancy in the newly combined organization. Because I had a law degree, I was moved into an entirely different department, which had little, if anything, to do with human beings—land asset management. I was now dealing with dirt—easements and right-of-ways. I still had a family to support and a mortgage to pay so I kept at it. Things like supporting a family were important—even if my job was killing me. At least if I died, I had some really good life insurance provided by the company.

After a year of trying to make this new assignment work, I was called in for a "chat" with my boss. In this chat, I was told I had six months to find a better fit and it was made clear that there wasn't a better fit for me at the company anymore. I wasn't able to keep pretending I could be happy or productive and it showed. At least I was given six months to find something. "Go with our encouragement and blessing, but go," I was told. "It is better this way for both of us." I wasn't just losing my job. We were breaking up.

Some people who knew how unhappy I had been told me I had been handed a gift by being let go, that fate or God was giving me a message and an opportunity. That's nice, I thought, but they weren't the ones who had to figure out how to make their next mortgage payment now that they were unemployed. So much for job angst, now I could start dealing with unemployment angst.

Each time a job I had ended (quit, laid off, fired, forced out, company failed, exiled, zombie apocalypse or whatever), I would once again gear up my pretend self and deep six all that creative "flakey" stuff. Each time I would say to myself, "Someday I am going to be true to who I really am, but right now I need income, health insurance, and maybe a few employee perks." Sure, I could ditch the family, run off to Costa Rica and live on the beach, but I actually liked having a family around. It wasn't just about obligation either. If I was going to live on a beach somewhere warm and sunny, I really wanted them to be there with me.

In my attempt to reconcile my right brain (the creative and "irresponsible" side) with my left brain (the logical and "responsible" side), I once again looked for something that I thought would do this. I still, however, wasn't going to be one of those flakes. My pride—and really, it was fear—demanded that I be a professional businessperson.

So once again, I tried to think of the most creative type of pursuit I could think of in the business world. I came up with entrepreneur. This wasn't the 1970s anymore when entrepreneur was a euphemism for "irresponsible deadbeat dreamer," (i.e., flake). Being an entrepreneur had risen in our society as the superstar of today's business world. They were cool, exciting, and rich—just like attorneys. I decided I would be an entrepreneur.

I was introduced to a mad scientist through one of the local university tech transfer offices. This mad scientist had come up with a wonder formula that had several potential applications in food preservation as well as some other interesting human health areas. It seemed like a great opportunity. This was not what I should have done. But entrepreneurship can be seductive–a siren call of potential wealth and mad-capped adventure. As I would learn from trying to get this business off the ground, more often than not, it is best to put wax in your ears and sail on past the sirens in your life to your true destiny–to be your true self. Sirens only lead you to shipwrecked careers. The venture didn't work out, in part, because I wasn't really excited by being in business. I wanted to write–but that was irresponsible.

In putting so much energy in trying to be what I wasn't, I never really considered or put a lot of energy into trying to come up with responsible or realistic options that involved right-brained types of jobs that I could do. Being right-brain oriented didn't necessarily mean I had to run off to a commune, sell handmade pottery items at county fairs or start voting Democrat. Not that I am knocking Democrats. I have always thought of myself as a moderate Republican, until I moved from Oregon to Utah. It turns out I am actually a Democrat– by the political standards of my new home state.

In the book, *A Whole New Mind: Why Right-Brainers Will Rule the Future,* Daniel Pink claims that although the last few decades have belonged to the left-brain dominated professions–MBA, lawyers, computer programmers–the "keys to the kingdom are changing hands." He asserts that the future belongs to the flakes, I mean right-brain thinkers. He cites examples such as creators and empathizers, pattern recognizers, artists, inventors, storytellers, and meaning makers– whatever a meaning maker is. It is these people who "will now reap society's biggest rewards and share its greatest joys." I think I will recommend to my sons that they major in meaning making–it sounds very promising.

If Pink is correct, which I am not sure he is–even though I want to believe–then those who find themselves predominantly right-brain thinkers should really have it made. The business world should be embracing these people with abandon. I wish! I am still waiting for the keys to the kingdom. In the meantime, I had to figure out how to be successful–meaning at a minimum, supporting my family and keeping a roof overhead–while being true to my right-brain dominated self. Before that, however, I needed to come clean with myself. I had to face the fact that I was a right brainer who had been pretending to be a left brainer.

The truth is that you use both sides of your brain. That our brains have this neat right-side, left-side dominance is one of those myths that have evolved. It's a simplification of studies done about what part of the brain is involved in different activities. It is a very convenient way, however, to explain how we lean, the way we swing–a shorthand for describing the dominant aspects of our personality. So why fight established wisdom, even if it's not really correct? No matter, and as they say in AA meetings, "Hi, my name is Jeff, and I am a right-brain dominated person." Okay, they don't confess brain region dominance in AA meetings, but they do say, "Hi, my name is…" The time had come for me to have the courage to come out of the right closet. Just don't expect me to be changing political parties. I am comfortable with being a moderate Republican/Democrat.

Although I have done a lot of article writing over the years, I have never considered myself a writer. Writers are, after all, in that category of starving flakey artists–except Stephen King, John Grisham, James Patterson, Danielle Steel, Dean Koontz, Suzanne Collins, J.K. Rowling, and a bunch of others. Okay, not all writers are starving. I won't even go into those who make a living as freelance writers. But they are the exception to the thousands who are "writers." I didn't think of myself as a writer. I was a lawyer or human resources professional who happened to write business related articles on the side. Yet, I loved writing. I needed to see myself differently–maybe not because I would earn my living as a writer, but because writing was what I actually loved. It was me.

See yourself for who you are instead of what you do for a living. What you do for a living can change. It might be your dream to matchup how you make a living with who you are. Don't, however, confuse who you are with what you do, as I did. Don't think you have to earn money at whatever it is that makes you, you. First accept who you are and then if your dream involves making a living at who you are, go for it. First have the courage to accept yourself for who you are.

What closet are you hiding in? Is it time you thought about coming out–even if only to yourself at first? You will need courage to do this, to face who you really are instead of trying to be who you think you should be. It is the first step in gaining the courage you need to grow.

✦ EXPERIENCE A GROWTH SPURT ✦

*Find the courage to be who you are
and resist the urge to run away.*

If You Aren't Good at Being You, Maybe You Should Practice More

Everyone wants to be an individual. The problem is that very few people want to be one by themselves.

How normal are you? Maybe even more importantly, how normal do you *really* want to be? There are actually a lot of good reasons why you might want to be normal. Society rewards normal people with good jobs, promotions, acceptance, and approval. Sure, we say we like rugged individualism—just not in our neighborhood. Then again, there are varying degrees of abnormal and we all have our limits of tolerance. For the most part, though, most people and corporate America would rather deal with normal people. Celebrate the out-of-the-box individuals, make inspiring commercials about them, but do not hire them as regular employees, they are a little too disruptive.

While in college, my aunt gave me one of those insulated pop can holders, the kind you put your can of pop or beer in to keep it cold. You see them in convenience stores and truck stops. Mine had the words, "Why Be Normal?" printed on it. I have often wondered this myself—"Why should I be normal?" I have kept that insulated pop can holder all

these years. It wasn't the first time someone came out and indicated I thought differently. If the opposite of normal was abnormal, then I wanted to be abnormal. I didn't want to be odd. I just didn't want to be normal like everyone else.

So why should you be abnormal? Because greatness, big dreams fulfilled, extraordinary achievement is about being abnormal–something other than how the majority thinks or what they do. Being odd on the other hand is its own category of personality traits that may have nothing to do with achievement. Thankfully my thoughts, or at least those I have been willing to share, have never branded me a heretic, got me accused of blasphemy, or tied up to a stake and burned–just the occasional veiled comments from relatives and others. Fitting in can be important but consider the difference between simply fitting in versus being connected with others.

Far too often we are willing to fit in as a way to be "connected" to others. Being a connected individual is important. Being a loner is miserable for most people–hermits being the exception. You can't accomplish as much or experience some of the greatest joys in life without being connected to people. When I was at Downtown Disney in Orlando, I saw the following quote by Walt Disney on a plaque, "You can design and create, and build the most wonderful place in the world. But it takes people to make the dream a reality." He was right. It does take people to make dreams a reality. You can still connect with people but stand out as an individual. When you do, you will no longer be normal–and that is a very good thing. It also takes a fair amount of courage to be willing to go there.

It can be hard being you–even under the best of circumstances. Most people, it seems, don't like themselves. Have you ever felt like there was something wrong with you that needed to be fixed? Oh, there are a few freaks out there. As Norwegian comedian Daniel

Simonsen points out, 90 percent of the population wishes they were somebody else. As for the other ten percent who really are happy with themselves, Simonsen says, "…those people are on cocaine."

Maybe you aren't really happy with who or what you are. Perhaps you have this list of things you would like to change about yourself. Maybe you really wish you were skinnier, and then you would feel better about yourself. Or perhaps if you had just finished college, you would feel better about yourself. Maybe you would like to be better looking, have stronger cheekbones or longer legs. Perhaps if you were more talented, could sing, play the piano, paint, or sculpt, you would feel better about yourself. Maybe you wish you were smarter, more clever, not shy, a better speaker, not be part of or come from a dysfunctional family, got along better with your relatives or in-laws, were a different race, weren't a minority, had straight hair or curly hair, or had hair, were more methodical, were less methodical, weren't so wishy-washy, were a better listener, weren't handicapped, weren't fat, weren't so old, weren't so young, had better motives for why you did things, had more money, had more talent or skill, and on and on it goes. There are countless ways that you may not be happy with who or what you are.

Most of us, it seems, want to be someone else. Depending on your dreams and desires, you may see a successful athlete, business figure, media personality, entertainer, or artist as the ideal person you want to be like. "If only I could be the next–whoever." We all have our "whoevers."

There were a lot of things I just wasn't very happy about when it came to who I was–and it wasn't even like I was a serial killer or even wanted to be one for that matter. Sure, like everyone else, I had the occasional homicidal thoughts aimed at certain well-deserving persons, but that was just fleeting fantasy and anger in the moment. No, thankfully I only had feelings of self-doubt, lack of belief in myself, imposter syndrome, shame, and feelings of unworthiness. Maybe it would have been easier to deal with homicidal tendencies, but that wasn't who I was.

I mistakenly thought I needed to be like these extroverted, gregarious, type A personality types if I wanted to achieve success in life. So I pursued a career that tends to attract those kinds of individuals, when I was anything but that. I believed this was how you became successful, never considering that the examples of success I was looking to were of a different breed than myself. I was so focused on who I wasn't, that I didn't pay attention to who I was, with all the great traits, strengths, talents, natural beauty, and attractive personality I possessed. It made me feel very out of sorts–like an ugly duckling. I was, however, a beautiful swan that didn't recognize it. Well, maybe not a swan, but some really cool bird like a hawk. Actually, I am a duck. I graduated from the University of Oregon–go Ducks! You get the point.

The legal profession wasn't the problem, why I chose the law was the problem. I am not singling out law, it just happens to be what I chose to go into. The problem is using a profession or job to make yourself feel okay while hiding from your true self–a self you may not like. James Franco explains it very well in the introduction of his novel, *Actors Anonymous*. Actors often have a self-hate that drives them to the stage, reasoning that if enough people clap for them, it will prove they are worthy of love and therefore they will love themselves. This concept isn't just about actors or lawyers. It's about you and me. If we hate who we are, why would we want to be us? No professional pursuit or applause will fix that.

As was established earlier, you must have the courage to face who you really are, which means you must become an individual. Individualism is a lot like creativity. We say we like it and want it, but when it comes to actually being an individual and having to stand alone, forget it. Most people want to fit in rather than stand out. You will have to stand out at some point if you are going to achieve your dreams. You can't continue to be like everyone else or the next "whoever." You will have to be you.

A trip to Costco made clear to me the importance of being you, as opposed to trying to be the next "whomever." Usually the only insight I get from shopping at Costco is that I would be wise to create a shopping list and stick to a budget. Like a lot of things I buy at Costco, insight wasn't on my shopping list. My shopping list usually just includes a fifty-pound bag of rice, a two-gallon sized Ketchup bottle, and a pallet of soy milk. My typical trips there involve spending my entire paycheck as well as the future inheritance of my children. I can't ever seem to "stay on list." The problem is that when I am there, I find about half a dozen other great things to buy that I had never even thought about. A trip to Costco is an exposure to opportunity–to acquire more material goods.

I have picked up a camping tent, air mattresses, bed sheets, a couple of area rugs, solar powered flashlights, office supplies, scissors, books, a portable folding table, shirts, socks, shoes, belts, and other sundry clothing items to name only a few of my "off-list" purchases over time. This list doesn't even include the various food items that have made it into my cart that were also never on my list. The thing is, if you don't get the items when you see them, chances are high they won't be there the next time you go back. You have to seize the opportunity then, or it may be gone the next time you return.

On this particular Costco trip there was an author selling and signing copies of his book. Sometimes I try to avoid eye contact with these authors. Sometimes when I am feeling brave, I will go up and talk to them. It was during one such time, when I was feeling brave, that I decided to talk to this particular author. I could gather from the cover of his book that the story was a young adult fantasy adventure story. As I approached the table where he was sitting, the first thing he asked me, before I could even say hello, was, "Do you know anyone who likes to read *Harry Potter* books?"

I was taken aback a little. I didn't see any *Harry Potter* books on his table. Nor did his book cover look like it was a book about wizards. Why was he asking me if I liked reading *Harry Potter*? I do like the *Harry Potter* books, but whose book was he trying to sell, his or J.K. Rowling's? Why was he trying to compare his book to her books? I could only gather from his question that this author was trying to imply that his book, like *Harry Potter,* was a wonderful and exciting read, a great adventure story with wizards and magic.

After chatting a little, I left him to his book hawking efforts and went on to spend money I didn't have on things that weren't on my list and that wouldn't be there the next time I came back. I didn't buy the author's book, but I got a copy of it to read from my local library a few days later (I am cheap like that). I had a suspicion that his book was not about wizards, although there might have been some magic involved. When I read the book, my suspicions were confirmed. His book had nothing to do with wizards.

But what if his book had been about wizards? Would I want to read a *Harry Potter* knockoff? No. I want to read something original, especially if it is a story about wizards. *Harry Potter* was not the first book about wizards, nor will it be the last. It was, however, original in how the story was told. I wanted to go back to this author and tell him to change his book pitch. He needed to be telling potential buyers how his story was original and exciting. Pitch his story, not J.K. Rowling's. She has enough money already. But, like so many of those off-list items I fail to get when I am at Costco, he wasn't there the next time I went back.

Your dreams and aspirations demand that you be original. From your DNA to your personality, no one is exactly like you. Even identical twins raised together have physical and psychological differences. Expressing our originality, however, is something few of us do. We would rather imitate or copy someone else, usually so that we can fit in. Or we aren't confident enough in ourselves to be ourselves.

Doug Stevenson is the founder and president of Story Theater International and the creator of *The Story Theater Method* for strategic storytelling in business. As a speaker, trainer, and consultant, Doug has coached and trained professionals from CEOs to entrepreneurs, including a member of the House of Lords in London. He has worked with the likes of Microsoft, Google, Caterpillar, and Volkswagen.

Doug has a saying that I picked up when I had a chance to work with him: "Love yourself and let them watch." Out of context, this could sound a little creepy–and get you arrested. He means be who you are, love who you are, because the real you is who we all want to see and be around. As his bio states, "Doug used to believe he was destined to be the next Bob Hope." Instead he "discovered that he isn't supposed to act like Bob Hope. His gift is the ability to give people hope." Doug knows what it means to be original, even though he started out wanting to be someone else. He discovered he had more to offer being himself. And so do you.

It's not that we can't or shouldn't learn from others. But regardless of the profession, trade, or undertaking, the ability to achieve your dreams often requires applying what you learned from someone else in your own unique way.

A few years ago, my wife and I went to a Billy Joel/Elton John concert. It was a fantastic evening of entertainment. Both have performed for millions and made millions. When you think about it though, both do the same thing, they play the piano and sing. Yet each of them has his own unique music and performance style, and that makes all the difference. At one point in the concert, Billy Joel had a chat with the audience. He explained that early in his career a music executive told him that there was already a piano-playing performer–Elton John. There wasn't the need for another one. But Billy Joel knew there wasn't a Billy Joel.

When I was in college, I went to a Beatles tribute band concert. It was an entertaining concert, but they weren't the Beatles. I can name all the Beatles, but I have no idea what the names of the members of the tribute band were. We remember the originals–not the copycats or mimics.

Having been to law school, I feel compelled to give a little legal lesson. In copyright law, the law protects the original expression of an idea. It does not protect the idea itself. In other words, ideas are for the taking, but if you can be original in how you go about expressing that idea, the law has your back.

There are thousands of stories, plays, songs, television shows, and movies–all based on the very same plotline. Take, for instance, the plotline of boy and girl meet, fall in love, face opposition, and in the end come to a tragic conclusion. Tragic love stories have their appeal. It is the plotline of the following stories:

- The story of *Orpheus and Eurydice*
- Lancelot and Guinevere in *Camelot*
- Anna Karenina and Count Vronsky in *Anna Karenina*
- Rhett Butler and Scarlett O'Hara in *Gone with the Wind*
- Tony and Maria in *Westside Story*
- Rick and Ilsain in *Casablanca*
- Rose and Jack in *Titanic*
- Romeo and Juliet in, of course, *Romeo and Juliet*

None of these stories would likely be confused with the other, even though each has the same basic plotline. Even so, each story is an original. Who knows what other stories will yet be told that will have this same plotline? If the story is told in an original way, however, it will stand out on its own.

There are billions of people in this world and yet very few express their uniqueness. We are starved for originals. When you decide to express your uniqueness, others take notice. Maybe you don't want to be a performer or be famous—not everyone does—although the whole fame and fortune thing seems like a good thing to me. But what do I know? That's just me. The important question is who are you? It takes courage to be you—and I mean that in the most complimentary way.

Oftentimes we sell ourselves short and therefore fail to live up to our full height (i.e., potential). Consider fruit—you know, bananas, apples, oranges—fruit. There are fruits and then there are superfruits, like açaí berries, dragon fruit and noni. What makes a superfruit so special? In a word, it's marketing. Sure, these fruits may grow in a part of the world you may have never traveled to, but so do bananas. In the part of the world where these superfruits grow, they are ordinary. According to Karl Crawford, a co-author of the book, *Successful Superfruit Strategy: How To Build A Superfruit Business*, "People think Superfruits are found just growing in an exotic forest somewhere. That's just not true—you can create a superfruit."

Bananas could have been a superfruit but Dole and Chiquita went for mass market appeal, made them ordinary and therefore sell for cents on the pound. Superfruit products, often sold in the form of a drink, go for dollars per ounce. Studies have shown that just about every edible fruit is very good for you. A few fruits, however, get anointed by multilevel marketing companies as having really special properties that will make you healthier, younger, better looking, and richer.

In reality, a superfruit is just a fruit that has had its unique nutritional properties emphasized and exploited. There should be a campaign to free exploited fruits. Maybe a benefit concert for them–Elton John could sing at it–I would go.

Think of yourself as a fruit–just go with it for a moment. You are full of good qualities and great potential. You, like every fruit, have the ability to be super. Do you have the courage to express your uniqueness, to be super? You already have uniqueness. You just need to quit hiding it and let others see you for who you really are. Since you are not a fruit, but a person (okay, some people are fruits and even nuts)– even so, you are the one who gets to decide your identity.

I received a Father's Day card one year from my parents. On the front was a picture of Clark Kent with his head bent, looking down at the ground. Behind him, filling the background was a picture of Superman in that classic Superman pose–hand on his hips, red cape a flutter. Superman was looking at Clark Kent. Of course Clark Kent is Superman. Mild mannered Clark Kent is the identity that Superman assumes to keep his real self, the superhero, from being known. The inside of the card originally read, "I wish you could see yourself the way I do." My parents had crossed out the word "I" in both places and replaced it with "We."

How often do you assume a Clark Kent kind of attitude, you choose to be a banana instead of a noni fruit? How often do you live your life as Clark Kent when you are really Superman? Me? Superman? You may ask. The answer is yes, you are! There is a superhero in each one of us, and the ability to live as such. You need to start acting and being who you really are, and quit assuming an identity that hides the superhero that you are.

Go ahead, be a superhero to yourself and to those you love. Have the courage to be the original that you are. I would, however, advise that you choose your superhero outfit wisely. Spandex isn't very forgiving or flattering on most of us–and underwear is usually best worn as under-clothing.

✹ EXPERIENCE A GROWTH SPURT ✹

Stop being normal and start being you.

You Can't Poke Out the Mind's Eye or Muzzle the Voice in Your Head

If you can't trust yourself, it's time you learned how. Otherwise your dreams will remain locked away where no one will be able to get to them, not even you.

We all have a voice in our head that speaks to us. It doesn't mean you are crazy–most of the time. (Some people have multiple voices that speak to them–they are crazy.) For the rest of us though, that crazy voice is what you should be listening to when it comes to deciding what will bring you happiness, because it knows–even if you are in denial about it.

You might think of that voice inside you as your spirit or your soul, your conscience or subconscious mind, your id or ego, your gut or intuition, a sixth sense or even the voice of God himself whispering to you–or even Jiminy Cricket. Whether you think of that voice in your head in terms of science or faith, philosophy or psychology, intuition or inspiration, each of us has experienced that voice, and it can be a guide to happiness or our worst enemy, depending on what we do about it when it speaks up.

Listening to it is important, so long as it's not in critic mode—putting you down and making you feel small, unworthy, insignificant, and lacking in ability. In that case, tell it to shut up and take a back seat in a bus driving over a cliff. Sometimes, though, it is telling you something that you should be taking seriously. True, it can be annoying, particularly when it points out to you your true desires and you know that you aren't doing anything about them.

When I shop at Costco, I almost always go by the book section. Every once in a while a book ends up in my cart, becoming another "off list" purchase. As I browsed the books, that voice in my head would speak up.

Inner Voice: "You would be very happy and satisfied if you were a succesful author."

Me: "Yes, someday I want to write a book, and see it for sale here at Costco, very cool indeed."

Inner Voice: "Well, that means you need to write a book."

Me: "Yes—that is true—and maybe a small, important detail. Actually, kind of an important detail to this whole dream, isn't it?

Inner Voice: "Yeah, kind of an important detail."

Me: "I really don't know if I have a big enough idea to write a book, though, something original enough. (I get a little whiny sounding voice in my head at this point). Would anyone really want to read it? I don't know anything about promoting or selling a book—other than don't tell anyone I write like J.K. Rowling. Writing a book that others would actually want to read is a really long shot. Afterall, I am not J.K. Rowling or Clive Cussler or Dan Pink or any other successful author I can think of."

Inner Voice: "Duh, no kidding you're not J.K. Rowling, you're not even a woman—and oh, you also don't write wizard stories. You know, however, that you won't be happy or satisfied until you have written a book. Do it. Come on, just do it. Write your book; don't try to be "whoever" you think you should be. BE YOU! You can do it!"

Me: "Yeah, I know, someday when it's right, I will. Oh, look! There are some new shirts over in the clothes section. I better go check them out before they are all sold out."

At which point I would do what I could to distract myself and get away from my inner voice, because it was annoyingly correct and I was be too chicken to do anything about it. I would finish my shopping, pay for what I had bought, and avoid thinking about the internal conversation I just had with myself. Actually, the voice would come back again, but this time as an inner critic—and foolishly I would listen.

Inner Critic: "You were totally right about not having a good enough idea for a book, or even something original enough. And yes—who are you that anyone would want to read it even if you did write it? And you made a very valid point. You don't know anything about promoting or selling a book. You were spot on about it being a long shot that anyone would want to read it. Seriously, who do you think you are? You can't write like a bestselling author."

I don't know how many times this scenario repeated itself, my inner voice engaging me in the same conversation and the follow-up one by the inner critic. Each time my gut would twist up because I knew what my inner voice was telling me, trying to get me to do, was what I really wanted to do. I knew it and I still didn't do it.

Your inner voice may not be telling you to write a book, but it is telling you something about what would really make you happy—and might be hard for you to do for any number of reasons. All those things my inner critic told me were also true—but didn't have to be—if

I was courageous enough to do what it took to pursue my dreams. The things my inner voice told me were correct about the things that were going to make me happy. I needed courage to act.

What would make you happier? What dream should you be chasing but aren't? Your inner voice is your best guide to the decisions you must make if you want to be happy and content in life. It has the answer and that answer really is as simple as deciding to take that crazy inner voice in your head seriously. You might not like what it is telling you, because you may be afraid to do what it's telling you to do. But it is urging you to greater things, to become a greater person. You may have a million reasons why you can't or won't do what it's suggesting, but it isn't wrong. Listening to it and doing accordingly will ultimately make you happier—unless it's telling you to kill people. In that case, get some psychological help... quickly.

It took me a long time to learn this lesson of trusting the voice in my head. The worst mistakes I have made in life have been not listening to it and not doing what it was suggesting. Take for example the summer between my junior and senior years at college. One afternoon, my friend Jerry called me and invited me to his family's beach cabin for the weekend. It wasn't a fancy place, but it was at the beach. What made that weekend so memorable for me was a discussion we had. In spite of it being summer, it was a cold windy day (if you know the Oregon coast, you know it can still be a cold windy day there even in the summer). We were sitting on a driftwood log discussing our future plans.

By this time, I had decided I would pursue law school. While we talked, I had the distinct impression that I was making the wrong choice about going to law school. My inner voice was speaking up, and speaking up pretty loudly—I could hear it over the wind. It was saying that I needed to stick with communications, my original major and career choice, even if I didn't know where it would lead me or how I would ever survive with the low paying job "I was sure to get" by majoring in communications. After all, law was a sure path to riches.

You might find it hard to believe, but not all attorneys are rich. Law can be a noble profession, in spite of what the Bible and other sacred writings have to say about lawyers. (If you are not familiar with what these various texts have to say about lawyers, let's just say that kinder things have been written about used car salesmen). A few lawyers are soulless and will likely end up with the Prince of Darkness for a room-mate in the afterlife. At least that is what my friend the politician believes. I don't even try to think about what happens to politicians in the afterlife.

As I have explained earlier, law is not a bad profession. I was at-tracted to the intellectual challenges you find in the study of law. It is also full of noble ideals. What other profession has taken on itself the responsibility to defend the down trodden and disenfranchised? What other profession strives to uphold such a lofty notion of justice for all? I wanted to be associated with such nobleness, Who wouldn't? Was it wrong that I just wanted to drive to the courthouse to carry out such noble deeds in a Mercedes? No. I was wrong for letting fear guide me, for not being courageous about who I really was and where my interests really were. So I ignored my inner voice that I had heard so distinctly on the beach and went on to become an attorney.

The results were that I was never really committed to being a lawyer. I didn't pursue a career in law enthusiastically. When you don't pursue something like a career with enthusiasm and commitment, it "ain't a good thing." It turned out that the lure of lucre didn't provide the kind of motivation I needed to excel and be engaged in the field of law. This lack of enthusiasm would unfortunately spill over into other areas of my life. That's what happens when you don't listen to your inner voice.

Glenna Salsbury is a professional speaker who speaks to audiences around the world. The late Zig Zigler was one of her personal friends. She was married to the late Jim Salsbury, a former Detroit Lion and Green Bay Packers football player. Not all of her associations have passed on, heavens no. She has plenty of friends still among the living, just some of them are now in heaven.

Glenna is so full of energy that she makes friends everywhere she goes. She describes herself as perky. When I met her she was seventy-one years old and had more energy than most twenty-year-olds. A phrase from a song by the rock band Queen came to mind, "dynamite with laser beams." It fits her personality.

I had an opportunity to meet and work briefly with Glenna after she spoke as a guest at the local National Speakers Association chapter that I attended. She extended a general invitation for those interested to meet with her the next morning for personal coaching. At the time, I didn't even consider doing it. I wasn't a speaker, professional or otherwise. I also had my job to get to in the morning. That night when I went to bed, however, I had an interesting dream.

In this dream I was interviewing for a job I was qualified for and really wanted. As I interviewed for the job, though, I came across as dull and boring and lacking in enthusiasm. I realized I wasn't going to be offered the job because indeed I was dull, boring, and lacking in enthusiasm. At that point in the dream, I woke up. It was 3:00 a.m. and I realized something. It wasn't just a dream–I really was dull, boring, and lacking in enthusiasm–not good traits to possess. Then I heard it, my inner voice. "Go to the coaching session with Glenna. You need it." I decided this time I would listen to it and do what it was telling me to do–it was a good decision.

Later that morning, at a more decent hour, when I got up to start the day, I made a change of plans regarding work. I called up the contact person for the coaching session and asked if there was still an opening with Glenna. There was. In the few hours I spent with Glenna that morning, I learned I could be something other than dull, boring, and lacking in enthusiasm. I had it in me to be interesting and enthusiastic–I had just been suppressing it. I knew there was a different person inside of me because I once met him–a person I call "New York Jeff".

A few years ago I went to New York City for the first time. I am normally a pretty quiet and reserved person in public. But in New York, I listened to my inner voice and went with it. I made friends on the street, as I was standing in lines or eating at restaurants. I got to know the people next to me while we waited in line to take the ferry to the Statue of Liberty. I made friends with a couple I sat next to while watching a Broadway play that Whoopi Goldberg was performing in–*Xanadu*. I hung out with this couple after the show while the wife waited for Whoopi to come out of the theater and sign a playbill. I made friends while seated with strangers at the Carnegie Deli for lunch. I can say I was inspired by New York City to be something bigger–to be taller–like the skyscrapers. I had a blast. I became New York Jeff.

As I walked around New York City, I noticed something, besides the grime. This was a city where the best of the best came and did their thing, the crème de la crème. Whether it is media, theater, art, finance, banking, advertising, fashion, law, or any number of professions or industries, even organized crime (not an endorsement, I am just saying…) some of the best in those fields are found in New York. I saw some of these people as they went about their jobs (not the organized crime types, thankfully). I saw the best being the best.

I witnessed a great example of this the day I had lunch at Smith and Wollensky, just around the corner from the Waldorf Astoria Hotel. I had been in meetings that morning and lunchtime rolled around. I was alone and didn't know where I was going to eat so I took a stroll and by chance came to Smith and Wollensky.

One of the first things I noticed when I walked in was the maître d' and the way he was interacting with each guest. Some of the guests were obviously regulars. I could tell from the dialogue that passed between them and the maître d'. It was like a reunion of best friends. Even those, like myself, who weren't regulars, were treated like old friends. This maître d' was the consummate host. The brief time he spent with me made me feel welcome and glad I had chosen to have lunch at that establishment. Was I comfortable? Was the food to my liking? Was there anything else I needed? Please, make sure to let him know and he would personally see I got what I wanted. This guy was on his "A" game.

I know full well that not every restaurant in New York City has that kind of service. There are bad restaurants with bad service. There is poverty, despair, desperation, ugliness, cruelty, injustice, shattered dreams, and a list of ills ten miles long that can also be found in that city. Even so, New York City is a place to which people come with their "A" game. It is a place where the best are being the best. I saw it in that maître d'. It is the Big Apple and those who want to be at their best are welcome to come and be their best.

My inner voice was energizing to listen to and follow. New York Jeff had experienced just how fun it was to take that voice seriously and feel the enthusiasm that came from doing so. Enthusiasm changed the way I saw the world and the way the world saw me.

When I came home, I was just Jeff again. My wife really wanted New York Jeff. I wanted New York Jeff. So what kept me from being New York Jeff? If New York Jeff would listen to his inner voice and go with it, why wouldn't regular Jeff? I had some serious Dr. Jekyll and Mr. Hyde stuff going on. Even if it would be a while before I could be

New York Jeff at home, I learned something important. If I trusted my inner voice, I could do and be things I wasn't normally inclined to do or be—yet were a part of me. When I had the courage to listen to my inner voice, the best of me came out.

Sure, there are times my inner voice drives me crazy, waking me up in the middle of the night telling me things I would rather not face or ruining a perfectly good trip to Costco. There is only one way to silence the crazy voice that prompts you to seek your dreams—do what it says. Of course when you do that, you still have to hear that annoying, "I told you so." Come to think of it, I am not sure your inner voice is ever really quiet. That's okay though. What is wrong with being your best self?

✪ EXPERIENCE A GROWTH SPURT ✪

Trust yourself, you're crazy not to.

Far Too Many People are Qualified to be the Village Idiot

You don't have to be a genius, just be willing to think.

What you think, what you fill your head with, is very important. Have you considered that how you think is equally as important? Intelligence is a function of what you do with what you know, not simply what you know. Being smart is great–I wish it were one of the traits I possessed. The real key to smart thinking, however, is learning to use a method to think with.

When I got out of law school my mother said to me, "You think differently than before you went to law school." I want to think she was referring to the skills in reasoning and logic I had developed over the three years of my law school experience. I wonder if that is what she really meant though. I have always had this nagging feeling she might have been inferring that my thinking had become a little odd. I will give her the benefit of the doubt though, since she is my mother.

Although law was not the profession for me, I have always been grateful for the way it trained me to think about

things and taught me how to reason through situations and issues. Reasoning and logic are good skills to have. They allow you to see situations in such a way that solutions can be found to problems. This ability has application not only in the law office, analyzing a client's case, but in life. It is very useful to be able to reason through difficult situations.

Good thinking is hard to do. Henry Ford supposedly said, "Thinking is the hardest work there is, which is probably the reason why so few engage in it." Even so, it can be much easier to do if you know a trick or two about what it takes to engage in better thinking.

I am going to let you in on a method for thinking through problems that is taught in law school—all for the price of this book, if you bought it. If you borrowed it from a friend or from the library then you get the method for free. In any case, you are about to save the hundred grand or so in books and tuition—not to mention the three year commitment it takes to get through law school. It is a secret guarded by solemn oaths and lots of Latin terms that no one is really sure how to pronounce. Latin is, after all, a dead language used mostly by lawyers who want to sound authoritative and expensive—as well as botanists, zoologist, doctors, and Catholic Priests during Mass.

You might think law students learn law in law school, and you would not be correct. They learn how to analyze the law in order to make conclusions, which is much more useful. You learn to analyze cases and law—the stuff of law school—using the IRAC Method (pronounced like the country Iraq). IRAC stands for **I**ssue, **R**ule, **A**nalysis, and **C**onclusion. The IRAC Method is used in law to analyze legal cases.

The black letter law, as they call the laws that are written, the statutes passed, and acts enacted, are really only a starting point. The real trick isn't in reading what the law says, but being able to take real-life situations and come up with solutions for your clients based on what the law says–more or less. High paying clients often encourage creative interpretations. If those real-life cases go to court, they become case law–which is the law we make up trying to solve a problem we never anticipated and so never got around to writing a statute for. In that case, the court makes a decision based on the lawyer's creative arguments and that decision becomes the law.

Take, for example the law, "Thou shalt not kill." It's what you would call black letter law. In this case it was first written on a set of stone tablets brought down from the mountain by Moses. Now, let's apply an IRAC analysis to a case in which someone has caused the death of someone else. I will keep the scenario simple.

In our case, Joseph the Israelite killed a Philistine while in a heated battle with the Philistines. The issue–the "I" part of IRAC–is whether or not Joseph the Israelite broke the rule of law–the "R" part of IRAC, "thou shalt not kill." Now comes the analysis part–the "A" in IRAC. You know that this was a war situation, an armed conflict sanctioned by the state. In that situation, a solider is not deemed to have broken the law when he kills the enemy. Joseph was doing what he was supposed to as a soldier in the Israelite army confronting the enemy–killing them. So what does that mean in this case? This is where you draw you conclusion–the "C" part of the C of IRAC.

In this case you conclude that Joseph the Israelite did not break the law "thou shalt not kill," even if he did in fact cause the death of another person, because he was a soldier in battle doing his duty in a war being conducted by the Israelite state against its enemies, the Philistines. In such a situation, a soldier is not deemed to have broken the law, "thou shalt not kill," when they cause the death of an enemy in battle.

Life is usually much more complicated. Even so, IRAC works very nicely. What if Joseph had killed his wife's lover after walking in on them in the middle of an adulterous relationship? What if he had killed the lover after careful plotting and planning? What if he had killed the lover in an accident when he and the lover got involved in a scuffle in which he had never meant to kill the lover, only throw him out of the house–but it happened to be the second story window? What if Joseph had hired someone else to kill the lover? You get the idea, lots of variations of the facts, but one law that you need to reconcile according to individual justice and society's needs.

You can use the IRAC method to think through situations in your own life, to think like a lawyer to solve your problems. It is a simple but very useful framework for thinking. Say for example your issue is that you want to start a business (the "I" of IRAC). Now ask yourself, "What rules apply to starting a business?" (the "R" of IRAC). You need to know about finance, taxes, marketing, your product, the customer and so on. Now ask yourself, how will I apply these rules to my business? (the "A" of IRAC). As you make a determination about what you will need to do–get a business license, obtain a loan, figure out how to market your services or product, and so forth, you are making your conclusions (the "C" of IRAC).

Years later, after law school, I went back to school for a degree in a science and technology master's program. My wife thought I was crazy–call it a midlife crisis. In retrospect, buying a red sports car might have been more fun. In any case, I was trained in the scientific method–another very helpful framework for thinking. The scientific method–making an observation, asking a question based on what you have observed, taking a guess at the expected answer, and seeing if you were right by testing out your guess–is a great way to learn and discover things.

There are variations on the scientific method, but the above summary captures the idea. Sometimes I consider the way I learned to reason in law as a method to solve problems and the scientific method as a way to discover new answers. In truth, both are very good methods of thinking that can be applied in a variety of situations to sharpen your own thought processes. Both methods provide helpful guidance as you think through situations and can make you look like a genius. And who doesn't want to be brilliant? Now you can be!

Neither framework is very difficult to learn and use. Both are a good method you can use to frame your thoughts for better results. Heck, the scientific method is so easy to learn, it is taught in grade school. There are other methods to clearer thinking for better results and you don't have to go to school for years–followed by years of paying off school loans–to think better. The trick is to actually use whatever method works for you–which I do about twenty-five percent of the time, on a good day, when the stars are aligned just so.

There is another aspect to thinking that is also very helpful when it comes to thinking creatively, "the box." There is much written about thinking outside "the box." As some of the most creative thinkers know, it's not about thinking outside the box so much as it's thinking about the box you are using. If you choose the right box, or framework, or set of rules, or values, your thinking can become incredibly creative. The trick is to choose your box wisely.

Take one of the most creative organizations on earth–Disney. As will become clear later, I have a thing for Disney, a good thing, even if they have taken a lot of my money over the years. Okay, I gave it to them willingly, and I am glad I did. Who doesn't love the parks and all those movies, and the Disney vacations? Now that that is out of the way, we can move on. Disney is very clear about why they choose to think in a box, a box made up of values that define the Disney brand. I have attended several presentations over the years by folks from the Disney Institute–their outside consulting group. In those presentations they have explained the box, or set of values, that they use to create all things Disney.

Disney's organizational identity, the box they use to think within, is defined by four components, as was explained at the annual Society for Human Resource Management convention that I attended.

1. Who is the customer, and what are those customer's attributes, likes, wants, needs, and so on?

2. What is the organization's vision? As in what do they aspire to be? Why do they exist?

3. What is their mission? In other words, how will they go about delivering on the vision they aspire to? What products, services, and experiences will they provide? If you have been to a Disney theme park, you know that an experience is a huge part of what you get there.

4. Finally, what is the essence of a Disney experience? What do they want their customers to feel when they are interacting with Disney, be it at a theme park, on a cruise, or at one of their world resorts?

Why does Disney think inside a box instead of outside a box? First, thinking inside a box of defined attributes provides a set of values, a framework that provides guidance for their efforts. Second, it keeps them from wasting resources–not even Disney has unlimited resources–unlimited pixie dust and dreams, yes, but when it comes to hard dollars they must determine what to spend them on. The third reason is that it keeps everyone focused on the things that make Disney, Disney.

There are other examples of boxes that allow incredible creativity, yet act as a guide to that creativity. Take the English alphabet. It has only 26 letters and yet by some counts there are over a million words in the

English language, with more being created every year. A piano has 88 keys. Think about the variety and number of songs written using only those notes. Actually, there aren't even 88 notes, just seven notes (not counting sharps or flats) that are repeated in different octaves.

Hollywood movie makers and writers all use a storytelling framework for creating stories, which at its simplest, consists of a beginning, a middle, and an end. There are, of course, more sophisticated constructs of the story framework–like the Hero's Journey–but the point is that stories are created within frameworks. True, when done poorly, the story is lame, and you regret you ever picked the book up or wasted your money on the movie. But it's not the framework or box that is to blame; it's the creator who missed, because when done right we love the book or movie. We will reread the book or see the movie again–maybe many times over. When a box is chosen purposely and with consideration, it will guide your creativity, not hinder it. It's how Emmys and Oscars are won.

Frameworks, boxes, and methods are all kind of in the region of logic and reason–left-brain stuff–yet they are an important part of creativity–right-brain kind of stuff. The best thinking we do is a synthesis of these different types of thinking. Actually, any effort at intentional thinking is a good thing. Or, as I once heard a nutritionist say about exercise, the best kind of exercise is the exercise you actually do. I would say the same goes for thinking, the best thinking may be the thinking you actually put the effort into doing. Heaven knows there are plenty who don't, especially among teenagers, other drivers you share the road with, those who don't belong to your same political party, and any politician regardless of political party (statesmen on the other hand–regardless of political party–do think).

You don't really have to be super smart, or even very smart for that matter, to think better. Thinking may be hard work, but it is well worth the mental sweat. You just need to learn a useful method and use it every once in a while. It will change the results you start to experience. And let's be honest, what good is better thinking if it doesn't get you better results in what you start achieving at work, at home, in your relationships? Isn't that what you want after all? Think about it. It's well worth the effort.

❂ EXPERIENCE A GROWTH SPURT ❂

Do the smart thing and learn how to think taller.

Four Letter "F" Words–
Fear and Fire

Walking on fire, it turns out, is easy.
It leaves you wondering what else might be
easier than you had thought it would be.

It takes real courage to think taller and be taller. How courageous are you? Most of us really never know or get the opportunity to find out–and we are okay with that. Like creativity and being an individual, we don't really like the process that gets us to the results, although we really like the end product. After all, courage is what results when you face what you fear, and very few people like to face what they fear. Facing your fears isn't fun, soothing or relaxing–like soaking in a hot tub would be. Facing what you fear is more like jumping in a lake of icy water.

The problem with fear, besides making you feel very uncomfortable, is that it stops you from doing a lot of things in life–at least it has me, I admit bravely. Fear has been a guide in my life. I'm not saying a "great" guide, but I would be lying if I said fear has not been a significant influence in my life, and perhaps it has in yours as well. This

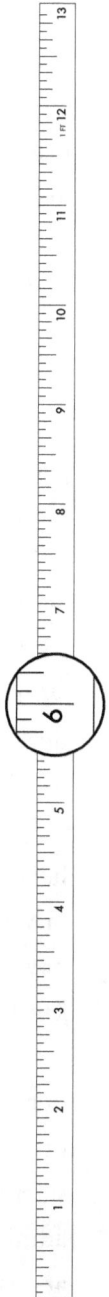

isn't a good thing, just in case you were wondering. True, you can avoid what you fear, but if you want to achieve your dreams, more than likely you will have to find just how courageous you are.

Fear comes in a lot of varieties and flavors. You might fear what others will think or how they will treat you, if they *really* knew you. You might fear you aren't good enough—either in a deserving sense or in an ability sense—to do or be, what you truly wish you would do and be. Maybe you fear you will let others down, or even let yourself down. Whatever your fear, it stops you from doing or being. Fear is like a traffic jam of the soul.

One day while reading the article, *The Storyteller*, by Erik Lunde-gaard, in *Mountain States Super Lawyers* magazine, I read a quote by Gerry Spence, the famed trial attorney, which I cut out and saved.

"I think we've been taught not to admit our fear, even to ourselves. We're all supposed to be brave. We're supposed to view our lives and those of our opponents without fear. But that isn't who we really are. We're all really very afraid. I think we have to recognize our fear and deal with it in an appropriate way. Once we face it and own up to it, it will energize us and, magically, it will retreat like a cowering dog."

Spence never lost a criminal or civil case from 1969 to 2010, and, yes, he was practicing law the entire time. He was very good at what he did, or very lucky, or very good at picking the cases he handled. I suspect, however, he was good at what he did because he understood people. He knew that we all have fears, but we can also deal with them.

For the record, however, let me say, it is a bad idea to show fear to a dog. Nor is it good to show fear to your enemies or bullies, at school or at work. Nothing good comes of it. They will trample you and consider it good sport. But Spence didn't say to show your fear, he said to admit it. Admitting it to yourself is what I think Spence was getting at—just don't show it to enemies or bullies—or dogs.

I had an opportunity to address this issue of fear head on one day by taking part in a fire walk. Right up front let me clarify something about me doing this fire walk… I am neither a daredevil nor a thrill seeker. I don't participate in extreme sports, because they are extreme. I don't like the feeling of immediate, impending, severe physical injury or death. I don't find that kind of thing exciting. I certainly didn't purposely set out to face my fears head-on by walking bare foot through fire. Like most people, I would have been content to continue ignoring my fears and avoid confronting them to the best of my ability.

It all started with my employment at an internet startup, back in the days of the dot-com boom. This is where I met Jamie. We were employees at SuperTracks, a digital music encryption and delivery start-up company. He was a project manager and I was the in-house attorney. I was actually in business affairs–the proper term for an in-house attorney in the entertainment and media industry. Oh, and it's not the industry either as I learned, it's The Biz–at least the entertainment aspect of it all. Our main office was in Portland, Oregon with a second office in Santa Monica, California–where all the music people were.

This was about as close to being cool as I ever got, or at least working in a cool place. It was fun while it lasted, your typical high venture dot-com start up. Lots of money raised, lots of money spent. Who needs revenue when you have venture capital? It's the same kind of thing going on today with all the apps for mobile phones being developed–lots of venture capital being poured into startups that don't even have a plan for making money.

We had a pool table in the lobby, all the free food we could eat, a stocked liquor cabinet, and even crazy employee theme days–like the fetish day. That one was "interesting" and I will leave it at that. It was a fun and exciting place to be. But the party ended when the bubble burst. We were out of money and out of business. Oh, and all those stock options I was issued? They would have been more valuable as toilet paper at that point. Internet start-up millionaire was not to be my fate.

Several months after the doors closed at this company I ran into Jamie. It turned out Jamie had this whole motivational thing going: a book, seminars, and fire walking. Who knew? As we talked and caught up on things, he asked, "Have you ever been to a fire walk?"

I, having never had such an experience, replied, "No, I haven't." At which point he invited me to come to one that he was hosting in a few weeks, to which I very enthusiastically replied that, "Yes! I would love to go."

I am not always quick on the uptake. I was thinking the whole time, "This will be really interesting to *see*." Honestly, I need to be more judicial about what I say "yes" to.

I didn't realize the participatory aspect of it until I arrived at the fire station–yes a fire walk at a fire station–and was asked to sign liability releases. This is when I began to experience fear–and it just got bigger as the night went on. It was a bit nerve-wracking to see the paramedic team with their medical equipment at the ready. You might think that seeing the emergency personnel would provide a little comfort, knowing that there would be immediate medical treatment if needed. The problem was that their presence only highlighted the fact that there might be a need for immediate medical treatment. There was also the local news with cameras ready to film the event. I signed my waivers and was off to the inferno. Well, not right at first. Jamie had a whole evening of fear inducing activities planned. We were going to face some fears that night for sure.

Several of the fire station personnel, including the fire chief, partici-pated in the events of that evening. Firemen had always struck me as rational people, especially when fire is involved. I have since changed my mind. Perhaps I should have known. My father-in-law, a former Santa Monica fire inspector, used to chase fires on his days off just so he could see what was burning and take pictures–for fun–with his young daughters in the car with him. It was the firemen who, with great enthusiasm, started to pour gasoline on the fire we would be walking over that night. "What was I getting into?" I asked myself.

It is often said that perception is reality. The first lesson we learned that evening was that your fears come from how you perceive what you are experiencing, not necessarily the experience itself. Your interpretation, which is colored by the preconceived notions or beliefs you hold determines how you will perceive what is happening. Our fears are made up of perceptions and those perceptions might be false.

We were told to take the word "FEAR" and look at it as an acronym–False Evidence Appearing Real. That's a good acronym. I also like–Forget Everything And Run–which was much more how I felt. The idea behind "false evidence appearing real" is that maybe what you experience has a different interpretation. If you can believe this, then it could change what you will do, or as we found out that night, what you can do.

Our first exercise in facing our fears was to karate chop a board in two with our bare hands. I wasn't too sure I could do this. I mean, come on, Bruce Lee I am not. Bruce Lee had years of training to do things like this. I had just walked in the doors of this fire station about a half an hour earlier with no martial arts training of any kind. I had visions of broken bones rather than broken boards. I even wondered to myself just how painful a broken hand would be and figured I just might find out. Actually, I did know what a broken hand felt like. I broke it playing a game of timed charades. I lost a round when the timer sounded, and in frustration, turned around and punched the wall and broke a bone. A broken hand doesn't feel great.

After some instruction and a demonstration by our instructor, one by one, each of us marched up to break the pine board we had been handed. "Look beyond the board," we were told. We were instructed not to look at the board–the obstacle–but to an envisioned place beyond the board. After seeing others do it, I figured I had a fighting chance at doing it as well. Thankfully, when it my turn came up to deliver a fatal chop to my designated board, the only thing I broke was the board. If Bruce Lee had been alive to see me do this, I am sure he would have given me an approving nod. I like to think so, at least.

The next activity involved walking barefoot on pieces of broken glass–sharp, jagged pieces of broken glass. We were instructed to let what we felt with our feet, what our body was telling us, not what we saw, guide us. "Don't look down at the glass, look forward to where you want to go and let your feet guide you." I let my feet guide me and I walked over that glass without getting so much as a nick. I was Superman, or at least I had the feet of Superman. I was feeling pretty good about myself. Good thing no one was passing out Kool-Aid that night–I am sure I would have drunk it. Heck, I *was* drinking the Kool-Aid.

I contrast this experience of walking barefoot on broken glass with one a few years later when I decided I wanted to try barefoot running. I thought it would be really cool, feel free and all, so I ditched the shoes. I ended up shredding my feet on the pavement. I couldn't run for a week after, even with my shoes on. Maybe I should have listened more to my feet that day. Running barefoot without toughening up the bottom of your feet takes more than trust. It takes thicker skin.

Our next lesson would be in the value of having a plan of action to help us face our fears. Of course it wasn't going to be something easy like writing out our goal on a piece of paper and listing the steps needed to reach it. We were apparently training for jobs in a traveling circus that night, so it had to be dangerous. It was, and it involved arrows–the kind used for target practice.

We were instructed to put the point of the arrow against the soft part of our throat. We were then told to put the other end of the arrow, the part with the feathers, against the cinder block wall of the fire station and hold it there without using our hands. We were then instructed, while keeping our hands behind our backs the entire time, to walk towards the wall until the arrow broke in two. Having paramedics there didn't give me any comfort when we did this exercise. I don't think a skewered throat falls under the category of minor injury, something treatable with a first aid kit. Thankfully, I completed the activity without the need for follow-up medical attention or the administration of last rites. My arrow snapped in two as I continued to advance towards the wall.

Just prior to this act of insanity, we had been told that by creating a plan of action and sticking to it, we were more likely to achieve our goals in the face of any resistance (like our fears) that we may experience. It doesn't have to be a complicated plan we were told. Ours wasn't. It was to keep walking towards the wall no matter how much resistance we felt–both from the arrow pressing into our throat, as well as the fear of serious injury–until the arrow broke.

It was suggested that our plans should be simple and that we needed to follow them in spite of the desire we would feel to stop. The arrow in our throat was the resistance. Keep walking towards the wall until the arrow broke in two was our plan of action. When it comes to highly charged emotional situations, like the pursuit of our dreams, a simple plan is usually best. Our lives are full of resistance to achieving our dreams. Thankfully, most don't involve the need for professional emergency medical personnel to be on hand. I keep the broken arrow as a reminder of what I did, and also that I don't ever want to do that stunt again.

Everything we did or learned that night was preparing us for the big event–walking through a fire barefoot. You might think that after doing all those other things, karate chopping a board in half, walking on broken glass, and breaking an arrow with your throat by leaning into them would pretty much eliminate any fears you might have about walking on a fire without shoes. This, however, was not the case. I was so terrified as we approached the fire. I was physically shaking.

As we stood, lined up to take our turn, we weren't told to be brave or to banish our fear. Rather we were asked if we believed we could do it. If we didn't believe we could, we were told we had better not try it because more than likely, we would end up burning our feet. We had been tricked. All those things we had done earlier weren't to make us braver. They were to get us to believe in what we could do. Being brave wasn't going to stop us from getting burned when we walked on the fire, but what we believed would. Belief in what we could do was going to make it possible for us to do it. "Why yes, of course, how very rational," I thought. Still, there was no turning back. I had come this far, I would do it.

Just a few moments before we were to take our walk, one of the firemen measured the fire's temperature. It was over 1300 degrees Fahrenheit. According to a famous short story, *Fahrenheit 451*, by Ray Bradbury, paper ignites at 451 degrees Fahrenheit. I don't know what it takes to burn feet, but it is something way below 451 degrees. The news people filming that night were pretty much guaranteed a story one way or another, a bunch of very burned people or an amazing display of bravery and belief.

I decided that night that I believed. At least I believed I could walk on fire. Before the evening was over, I would do it twice. The first time over the fire, I walked about as fast as I could just to get it over with. But once I had done it, I felt exhilarated. When asked if there was anyone who wanted to do it a second time, I got in line. I wanted to prove to myself that I really had done it, that it wasn't just a one-time trick. In fact, on the second walk, the instructor actually became concerned that I was taking too much time in the fire pit. He was at the other end with a very worried look imploring me to walk a little faster. Why did he care? I had signed my liability waivers.

There are several scientific theories that explain how people can walk on red-hot burning coals and not be burned. They range from the Leidenfrost Effect (which has do with a thin barrier of moisture being formed between your feet and the coals), to the heat conductivity of one's skin. Blah, blah, blah. It's the people who aren't comfortable with things that look a little irrational or that are so emotionally driven that want to explain it all away with a theory.

I am not saying there isn't a scientific explanation, but there are also some very powerful lessons in the experience. Even the skeptics and naysayers who have participated in fire walks have a belief in their ability to do it. They may not believe it has anything to do with all the hype or woo woo stuff—being in touch with your inner self and such is usually taught at these kinds of events—but they do believe they can walk on the fire and not get burned. Belief is extremely powerful—more powerful than fear or skepticism. If you wait to start pursuing your dreams in earnest until you are no longer afraid of whatever it is that you are afraid of, you will never start and you will never obtain them.

I learned a lot of great lessons that night: be careful of what you enthusiastically say yes to; just because everyone else is doing it doesn't mean you should; avoid former colleagues who are into motivational stuff; doing crazy stuff is crazy; and that walking on fire is easy but it takes real belief to walk on fire. I also picked up some great skills, all of which will come in handy the day I decide to join the circus–which I don't think is really a bad idea some days.

I also learned some great lessons about looking to the goal and not at the obstacle, trusting yourself, and having a plan of action. What I really learned that night, however, was that belief is real. Belief is really, and I mean *really*, important. It precedes knowledge and is what will give you the ability to act–even in the face of your greatest fears.

When that night was over, I wasn't free of all my fears, but what I believed was possible had changed. If you can change what you believe, you will have the courage you need to chase your dreams and achieve your goals–at least if it involves pine boards, broken glass, arrows or burning infernos. I suspect it applies to a few other areas of life as well. Belief is the root of courage and a much better guide in your life than fear–and that is a good thing, just in case you were wondering.

❁ EXPERIENCE A GROWTH SPURT ❁

Face your fears with courage and belief, even if you must close your eyes to do so.

If We Were Meant to Run Naked, We Would Be Born That Way

Run for something, even if it's just so you can eat another bowl of ice cream, but run.

How do you become something? How do you become the person you desire to be, after you have come to terms with the person you are? Simple. You work at it, consistently, persistently, until one day, you wake up and you have become that person. Easy enough. It does take work though, which is why so many people never seem to get there. With enough of a reason, however, you can do it. I learned this by accident on the day I realized that I had become a runner. Who knows what you will become or do if you work at something consistently with persistence?

I used to run when I was younger, back in the days when I didn't need the exercise, but had the energy to do it. It was the late 1970s and jogging was a very popular activity. Some liked it so much they did it nude. You may recall the streaking craze. There was even a popular song about streaking. My guess is that the runner's high was behind streaking– that euphoric feeling one gets from hard physical exercise.

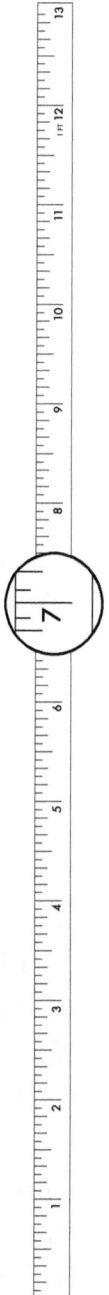

Well, that and narcotics. It was the 70s after all. People do crazy things when they are high.

I was in junior high school at the time. I never did see anyone streaking, much to my disappointment. The idea of seeing someone running naked appealed to my adolescent mind. The realities of seeing someone running nude now makes me want to think of something else very quickly. Personally, I always kept my clothes on when running, runner's high or not.

A few years ago I decided to get back into shape. My hometown is Beaverton, Oregon which is also the headquarters of Nike Corporation. Running is in the air in that part of the country. Even though I no longer live in Oregon, it was natural that I should go back to my roots when deciding what exercise I would take up.

Running has a long and storied history. The first person to run a "Marathon" was Pheidippides, a Greek soldier, who ran to Athens from the Battle of Marathon with the good news that the Persians had been defeated. After reaching Athens, the exhausted Pheidippides gave his message, collapsed and died. Fortunately, the vast majority of runners don't collapse and die these days. Running is supposed to be associated with good health and energy, not exhaustion and death. Then again, Jim Fixx, the man who is given credit with popularizing running as an exercise didn't fare too well either. He died of a heart attack at age 52 while out on a run. Perhaps running has its drawbacks. Even so, I decided to start running again because it makes me feel alive—all beat-up afterwards—but alive.

My first pair of real running shoes when I was a kid were Nikes, of course. They were banana yellow and a bit too big for me. I picked them up at a warehouse sale, the kind Nike would occasionally have back in those days to liquidate inventory. It was also at one of those warehouse sales that I picked up another pair of Nike running shoes for $5.00 that I still own. The uppers are made of orange leather and a green nylon. They wouldn't be considered too fashionable today, nor were they really very fashionable then, either. I am guessing it's why they were at the warehouse sale. They are so simple in design and construction compared to what running shoes have evolved into today.

The only thing I did in preparation before I took up running again was to buy a new pair of running shoes. I went for something with gel in them because I had some vague idea about cushioning and shock absorption. I really didn't know much about what I should get in a running shoe as they had evolved quite a bit technically, but gel seemed like a good thing to have. They were Sauconys. They fit nicely, and were on sale. "On sale" is often a requirement for whatever exercise gear or clothing I buy. These days I am back into Nikes– I think they make me run faster. When I bought them, it was kind of like coming home, and no, they weren't on sale. There are always things about yourself you can change–like not being cheap all the time.

So I got my new running shoes and, as the Nike slogan challenges, I just did it. I didn't bother buying any new clothing or equipment. I didn't even read about running techniques or styles. I figured gel was good enough. It wasn't until I had been running for over a year before I had even heard the word "pronate." When I would tell people I had decided to start jogging, all these serious runners would start talking about pronation and buying the right kind of shoe. I had to look up the word to find out what they were talking about.

According to articles I read, knowing how much your foot pronates is essential to choosing the right kind of running shoe. I didn't let my ignorance stop me. I suppose I pronated for well over a year before I bought my second pair of running shoes–with expert help. They had me run on a treadmill while they watched to see how I was placing my foot and how much I was pronating.

I said I started to run because I wanted to get back into shape, which is true, mostly. The real reason, however, the thing that motives me and keeps me going, is that I like eating ice cream. I like ice cream a lot. Just ask me about eating it at the right temperature so you enjoy its full flavor bouquet, butterfat content, air content, ice crystal inhibitors or binders–I think you get the picture. Ice cream also has a lot of calories–at least the stuff worth eating does.

Oh sure, I wanted to be healthy and fit, and all of that stuff– at least that is what I tell others. I am embarrassed by my real motivation for exercising. Since I am already short and bald, I can't bear the idea of being fat too–and so I decided I had better exercise. I figured regular exercise would allow me to keep eating ice cream like I was still a teenager. As for the idea of moderation in my ice cream eating habits, please, be serious. Don't get me wrong, I really like being in shape. But being in shape alone would not have kept me out on the streets running day after day, in heat and cold, in sunshine, rain, or snow for the last four years. Vanity and gluttony, on the other hand, have.

My two sons and I ran a 5K the other day. It involved obstacles to climb, crawl through, go around, and zombies. The zombies were the best part. Now that's motivation to keep moving–having the undead chasing you. Unfortunately, fear of being eaten by zombies can only keep you motivated for so long. What do you do when the zombie apocalypse is over? Personally, I would celebrate with a big bowl of ice cream–which would motivate me to go for a run. A win, win situation if you ask me.

The point I am making is that if you want to make a change in your life, you will need to find something that keeps you motivated over the long haul to keep at it. You must be consistently persistent. It's going to get rough at some point, no matter what you decide you want to accomplish. Writers like Seth Godin and Steven Pressfield refer to the resistance, the force that is out there and works against you any time you try to accomplish a dream or make a change in your life. You need to find something, some reason to keep going at it in spite of the resistance. Mine was a desire to continue to eat ice cream in large quantities without becoming large (I wanted to be taller, not larger). It worked for me. I would have liked to do it for noble reasons, but truth worked best for me.

When I started to run again after all those years of not running, it was really more of a shuffle on my part, something like how zombies move in the movies–well it depends on the movie. Some of those zombie movies make the undead run like super-beings. What is with that anyway? Those people, now turned zombies, never moved half as fast when they were alive. Zombies are supposed to amble and shuffle. Being undead doesn't make you faster–that's what new shoes are for.

Anyway, I would go running (i.e., shuffling) on routes that would take me outside of my neighborhood. I didn't want anyone I knew to see me. I looked pathetic. My goal was a simple one–run–or at least keep a constant forward movement for at least 25 minutes, three times a week.

I was out of shape when I began and also in awe that I could feel so much pain while doing something that was supposed to be so good for me. No wonder people died running. It took some time, but eventually I started to get into it. As I kept at it, the pain started to decrease and my lungs didn't feel like they were going to explode every time I went for a run. I even started to look like I was a competent runner. This, however, may have been due to the new running clothes my wife bought me. I guess after I proved my commitment, she decided I should look better as I ran on streets where I could be seen by neighbors.

When people know I run, they often have all kinds of advice for me. Their suggestions often involved buying lots of expensive monitoring equipment that I should be wearing, stuff to keep track of my heart rate, my pace, overall time, distance, altitude, calories burned–current stock prices, whatever.

I have been given advice on when I should run or not run. What surfaces to run or not run on. How I should eat, when I should eat, what I shouldn't eat. I have been told I should run in the mornings and I have been told I should run in the evenings. I should run this race or that race, and on they go. I find it interesting how many authorities there are on the subject, and how many of them don't even run.

I am not into all of this. I just want to get out, run my route and enjoy the time doing it. I now find running to be more of a mental pleasure than a physical one (not hard, admittedly). Running provides a time for me to think, to clear my mind, and even to meditate. It is one of the reasons I don't really like to go running with someone else, it's my alone time. The other thing I really enjoy when running is listening to podcasts of NPR's Science Friday. I get my science fix. You can't listen to a podcast and run with a buddy–it's too antisocial and weird.

My running gear consists of an iPod Shuffle for listening to Science Friday podcasts. If it's nighttime, I wear a reflective vest and a clip-on light that flashes. I figure after my neighbor almost ran me over the other day I should make myself a little more visible for those evening runs. She claims she didn't see me in the dark. I am still not sure what to think about that. These days I take more care in the shoes I run in– I don't want to be over pronating. I also wear a metal tag on my shoe that gives emergency contact information on it, just in case I end up finishing my run like Pheidippides–or get hit by a neighbor's car.

Some days I have wondered if I am running *from* something, *to* something, or *for* something. Or maybe I just want another bowl of ice cream. There have been times, and still are, when I do not feel like going running. It's too hot or it's too cold or I am too tired or I just don't feel the love. Sometimes, I will feel pretty good after getting out. Other times I come back from my run and the only good thing about the run is that it's over—and that I left the house in spite of how I felt. I have learned that sometimes action must trump how you feel that day. Sometimes, it just comes down to committed persistence when you want something. There are times when how you feel isn't relevant to making something happen—rather it's about whether you get up and do what needs to be done or not. After all, action ultimately counts, not intentions.

W.H. Murray was a mountaineer who climbed mountains all over the world. He was also a writer. You have probably read or heard the following quote by Murray. It's quite inspirational and a bit romantic. (He also misquotes Goethe but hey, it is still a powerful statement and Goethe should have said it that way anyway).

"Until one is committed, there is hesitancy, the chance to draw back, always ineffectiveness. Concerning all acts of initiative (and creation), there is one elementary truth, the ignorance of which kills countless ideas and splendid plans: that the moment one definitely commits oneself, then providence moves too. A whole stream of events issues from the decision, raising in one's favor all manner of unforeseen incidents, meetings and material assistance, which no man could have dreamt would have come his way. I learned a deep respect for one of Goethe's couplets: 'Whatever you can do or dream you can, begin it. Boldness has genius, power and magic in it'."

Murray joined the Argyll and Sutherland Highlanders when World War II started. His unit was stationed in the Middle East and

North Africa. In June of 1942 he was captured by the Germans during a retreat of his unit and spent the rest of the war as a prisoner of war. It was during this time that he wrote the manuscript for a book. He wrote it on the only paper that was available to him, the rough toilet paper they were rationed in the camp. The manuscript was confiscated and destroyed by the Gestapo. So he started over.

Life wasn't good. He and his fellow prisoners of war were living on a starvation diet in very poor physical conditions. There was no guarantee that he would survive or that his manuscript wouldn't be confiscated and destroyed again. But he did survive and the war ended in 1945. In 1947, Murray published his book, *Mountaineering In Scotland.* It was the first of three he would publish. In 1957, he wrote a sequel to his book, *Undiscovered Scotland.* It was his third book, *The Scottish Himalaya Expedition,* about his 1950 climbing expedition to the Kumaon mountain range in the Himalayas that contains his now famous quote.

What if Murray had not persisted? What if he didn't rewrite his first book after the manuscript had been destroyed by the prison guards? Would there have been a second or third book–the one that has his famous and inspirational quote in it? What magic awaits your efforts? Is it worth finding out? Is it worth being bold?

Being bold should not be confused with doing something big, grand, or impressive. The truth is that most things we have to do to achieve our dreams aren't so glamorous, let alone big, grand or impressive. They are often small and even tedious but if done with consistent persistence, they get the job done. The end results are what will be impressive, even if the process of getting there isn't.

This isn't a quick or glamorous way to accomplish things, but it works and it works very well. The trick is sticking with things. Therein lies the problem as to why so many don't achieve their dreams. They aren't willing to be committed and persistent over long periods of time, years even.

Most of us want things to happen quickly. We don't want to have to keep at it. We would rather put out a grand effort and be done with it. Your dreams, however, often require a lot more than a grand effort. They require sustained effort. Small actions taken consistently will often net bigger results than big actions taken sporadically and unsustained over time.

Often we think that if we can't accomplish our dreams within a week, we don't have the ability to accomplish them at all. This conclusion is tragic because the reality is that just about everyone has the ability to accomplish their dreams if they will be consistent in their efforts and persistent.

I have been running consistently for years now. A friend of mine once asked me how my running was going. I told him how I had been getting out consistently for a couple of years now and was up to so many miles a run. His response to me was, "You have become a runner, Jeff!" You become what you do. I became a runner by running. I have also grown rather fond of that runner's high. I am still not going to run naked, though.

🔆 EXPERIENCE A GROWTH SPURT 🔆

Keep running to your dreams until
you get there. Experience is not required.

Performance is Really Just an Act

Life is usually not scripted, so get comfortable with improvisational acting.

There can be no show—or anything to show for that matter—unless you act. No matter how tentative your steps or bold your leap, you must do something if anything is to change in your life—be it the way you think or the things you do. In theater, when actors fail to perform, there is no show. In life, when you fail to perform, you end up with nothing to show for your dreams.

A couple of years ago, I decided to take an improvisation (improv) acting class. It was a tentative step toward accepting that I was really more into all those creative kinds of things than I was admitting to. I justified these acting classes by figuring I could learn some good communication skills—very useful for a career. I also wanted to have some fun. Secretly, I wanted to become a famous actor. Of course I never told anyone about the wanting to become a famous actor—do you think I was crazy? In any case, two of my three reasons for taking the acting improv classes happened—I did learn some good communication skills and I had fun. My backup

plan for number three, become a famous actor, was to live my secret dream vicariously through my son.

Many fathers had a childhood dream about being a basketball, football, or baseball star, playing in the Pros. So when their son starts playing sports, it's an opportunity for them to live the dream vicariously through their son. Not me—at least not me when it came to sports. Rather, I had this dream of acting, so why shouldn't I live my unrealized acting dreams through my son's theater involvement? Pathetic, I know. We are all delusional given the right circumstances. My son ended up not taking to acting. His interests migrated to computer programing, which it turns out he is pretty good at. Maybe he will write some new program and make a ton of money. Perhaps rather than living my acting dreams through him, he can provide me with a retirement when he makes his millions as a hotshot programmer.

I learned improvisational acting from Eric Jensen. Eric is a cofounder and the Artistic Director of the Off Broadway Theater in Salt Lake City and has been acting for over 30 years. People take his classes for a variety of reasons, some to actually get into performance, others, like myself, who were still in the right-brain closet, "to learn some transferable skills." Wink, wink.

It turns out that you really do learn many useful skills in improvisational acting. Improv is even used to teach corporate group skills like effective communication, adaptation, teamwork—how to make people laugh. Don't discount the skill of making people laugh. It is extremely helpful and much needed in the workplace.

One of the things I learned in the class was if you are in a scene and are having trouble coming up with something to say—remember, this is improvisational theater, no scripts—often moving to a new location or into a new position will trigger a new thought. It is more than a change in stage geography, though, that does this. The very act of moving itself gets the mind moving as well. There is definitely a connection between thought and physical movement. One of the principles is the power of movement. Nothing happens on stage when you are standing still—or in life for that matter.

Creativity needs movement. Creativity breeds new opportunity from forward movement, building on what has come before even as it produces something entirely new and different. The thing is that new and different often won't come unless things are moving—be it dialogue on a stage or opportunity in life.

Movement provides you with new perspectives. It puts you in places where you might discover things you hadn't noticed before. It puts you in contact with new stimuli, new ideas, and other people. It gives your brain something new to work with. It also gives you courage. Movement is critical to improvisational acting and can be used to great effect in helping you achieve your dreams.

What does movement look like in life? Sometimes it's an actual physical move in geography, like moving from Wyoming to Florida, or from the west side of town to the east side of town. Some of the best moves, however, are those that involve doing something that you had not been doing before. Like deciding to take a class in something you always wanted to learn how to do—or secretly wanting to start a new career but aren't brave enough to admit it. I am just saying…

One of the things I have often done as a result of my fears in life is to think in "but" terms—as in, "I would like to do acting, *but* it will never lead to anything." "I would like to change my job, *but* what I have now is secure." I would like to start a business, *but*…" You learn a very important antidote to "but" thinking in improv, it's called the "Yes, *and*…" principle.

The "Yes, *and*…" principle works this way. Whatever your fellow actor might say to you, or whatever scenario they present, you are to respond to it positively–often best done by saying "yes." After affirm-ing what the other person has said, it is then your opportunity to build on what they have given you. Hopefully into something funny–it is improv after all. The word "and" opens doors. It creates an environ-ment where the mind is now thinking in terms of "What is next?"

"And" is the opposite of "but." The word "but" shuts down the thought just expressed as opposed to expanding on it. It puts a stop to things. It's a judgment. The word "but" doesn't invite one to think of what is next, it's like a period to that particular thought. The use of the word "and" continues the dialogue and opens new avenues for explo-ration–even if those avenues are non sequitur and silly, which makes for good theater and funny results. It also makes for an interesting life. Believe me, I know what living a non-sequitur life is like.

By thinking in terms of "and," you start thinking of what is next and what could be. You are setting yourself up to think of more ideas, thoughts that are in addition to what has just been said. It both reveals and creates possibilities. Thinking in terms of "and" is the mental equivalent of physical movement. It puts your mind in a place mentally where you can see new perspectives. Perspective is key to seeing the opportunity that surrounds you.

Another great principle I learned in improvisational acting was that you must be willing. Willing to head straight into a situation in which you have no idea where you are going, let alone how you are going to get there. Willing to do it no matter how afraid or embarrassed you think it might make you feel. Willing to try–willing to stand there naked–metaphorically–in front of an audience and not run away–because that would be streaking–metaphorically. Willing to give it the best you have at that moment–to jump off the cliff and into the unknown. We were told that if we could do that, we would be surprised at what we would learn about ourselves and what we could accomplish. Instead of falling to our deaths, we would find our comedic wings.

What Eric was telling us, in improvisational theater speak, was that you have to be willing to take emotional risks. These risks are the hardest to take, on stage or in life. In life you must also be willing to do these things for your hopes and dreams if you want them to come true.

A few years later I was at a Christmas dinner program. The entertainment for the evening was Mike Rayburn, a comedian, world-class guitarist, and inspirational speaker. Mr. Rayburn posed two questions to us that night, "What if?" and "What would it take?" Two simple questions meant to be asked without judgment, an invitation to simply consider what could be if we just let ourselves imagine a little.

These are the worst kind of questions because if you let them, they will turn your world upside down. These are the kinds of questions that lead a person from a sane, safe, and all-is-right-in-the-world place to radical thoughts, anarchy, and chaos. Oh, Mr. Rayburn looked all innocent and harmless as he played his guitar and sang his funny songs, but he was an agent of bedlam.

I was sitting at a table with some of the other chapter members, making small talk. I was there stag–my wife doesn't enjoy dinner parties where she doesn't know anyone and has to pretend to like making small talk. This was my thing, not hers. I got into a conversation with one of the wives in which I mentioned that I had taken improv acting classes.

She asked me if I wanted to act. "Yes, I would," I said, almost without thinking. "I think it would be a lot of fun." At this point, our conversation moved to some other topic. At least our conversation moved on. My mind didn't. I was stuck in what I had just said to her. "Yes, I would like to act." Why had I said that to her, out loud? Well, being under the influence of Mr. Rayburn and his funny songs, I asked myself those two questions he had posed, "What if I pursued acting? What would it take?"

I went home that night thinking about the answers to those two questions. What would it take? Hypothetically speaking, of course. I could try out for a community play. I might have a fighting chance at a part even if I had no experience–after all, how hard could acting be? Don't you just get up on stage and act all dramatic? As I thought about it more, I considered acting classes; the kind real actors go to learn their craft. But I lived in Salt Lake City, not New York or Los Angeles. Maybe there was something locally. I didn't know. I decided to see what I could find.

You may not know it, but a lot of movies are filmed in Utah, from westerns to contemporary films. Some of the more famous contemporary ones are *Footloose, Thelma and Louise, High School Musical, The Lone Ranger, Pirates of the Caribbean: At Worlds End.* Several Television shows have also been filmed in the state, including *Touched by an Angel, Everwood,* and *Promised Land.*

I found the kind of classes I was looking for, taught by a legitimate, real life veteran of film and stage living right here in Utah, Michael Flynn. Michael has been in numerous films, television shows and stage productions in Utah and L.A. He is also a producer. So I called Michael up, asked him about the classes he was offering, and signed up. I didn't know what to expect. I got a few emails that were full of quotes and promises, all themed around what we would experience– frustration, joy, hard work, sweat, tears, and laughter–real "passion-of-life" stuff. All very dramatic, just like I thought it would be. I could hardly wait to start. I was ready to perform.

The classes were held in a studio-type setting, an all-black square room. Lighting hung from racks in the ceiling. One wall had posters on it from movies filmed in Utah. The opposite wall was full of head-shots from actors who had taken the class. In the middle of the room sat a camera, usually focused on a single chair. This is where the work took place.

I thought acting would be easy. It turns out I was wrong–so very wrong. Yes, there are those people–just like with anything else–that have natural talent and ability… and I hate them. Okay, not really–I am only jealous. Then there are the rest of us who find out that what looked so easy actually involved a lot of skill, skill that had to be learned and developed. What looks easy in acting is the result of a ton of practice and work–as if this should be surprising. Often all we see is the end result of effort and not the effort put into getting there, so we mistakenly think it would be easy to do something–like act in front of a camera.

I met some very fun and interesting people who were quite serious about their craft. They weren't into being "all dramatic," as I had mis-takenly perceived actors to be. Among my fellow students were some real actors, people who had been working in the industry and had significant roles in movies. One of my fellow students had been a ma-jor character in the Disney *High School Musical* movies and had been living and working in L.A. recently. This was a real acting class with real actors, who were really good. I was so in over my head.

The situation was a bit intimidating and it provided me with a real incentive to be prepared when I came to class. Often I would think I was very prepared. I would have my lines memorized. I had prac-ticed saying them in different ways, with different motivations behind them. I would then get to class and forget my lines as soon as I was in front of the camera. My mind would freeze. Apparently, invisible mind freeze rays would shoot out of the camera rendering me stupid. When I did remember my lines, I looked like I was acting. You aren't supposed to look like you're acting—that is a bad thing. You are supposed to look natural, not forced or staged. As I mentioned before, it's a lot harder than it looks.

I worked hard, which is always a good idea, especially when you have little to no talent. I actually started to improve as the classes progressed—not hard to do when one starts so low on the talent scale. I learned a lot about real life from pretending, or rather acting. This is because to be a good actor, you must be a good observer of people and the world around you. You can't convincingly portray what you haven't observed and somehow internalized.

Surprisingly, none of this discouraged me. I wanted to come back. I wanted to do better—even after viewing my videotaped performance the next day. The video was made available to us via a password protected (thank goodness) website. It was challenging and rewarding. I loved it. I got better, although maybe not great, and I will always be glad I took the class.

Soon after taking the classes, I got a small nonspeaking part as a paid extra in a locally filmed television series, *Granite Flats*. I played a factory worker in Russia on November 22, 1963, the day President John F. Kennedy was assassinated. I walked out of a building, right towards the camera. It turned out that I was in the final five seconds of the season finale. You could actually see me in my long winter coat and big furry hat in those few seconds. I was pretty happy. Was it my big break into show business? No. Dang. But I did it. I went and took acting classes and got a part in a show—even if only for a few seconds—and had a blast doing it. Out of the closet and on to the small screen!

In his book, *You Can Act!*, D.W. Brown wrote that the biggest obstacle to an actor is his or her inability to let go. He explains that most actors are too afraid to become vulnerable. They want to remain safe. It doesn't work that way, according to Brown. He compares great acting to riding a bull. If you really want to be a great actor, you must be willing to ride this bull. What bull are you facing when it comes to what you dream about doing or being? Does it terrify you so much that it is kicking your butt before you have even jumped on its back for the ride of your life?

More often than not, instead of facing that raging bull, I have opted to ride a pony. Pony rides are safe. They are distractions, activities you engage in that allow you to fool yourself or others into thinking that you are indeed doing something about your dreams—the writer who is always writing but never finishing anything or submitting their work (so I understand from a "friend" of mine); the person who is always putting together a business plan but never takes out a business license; the person who thinks about getting a degree but never enrolls in classes. I have known people like this and you probably have as well. They are constantly busy doing things, to get ready to do the thing they mean to do someday. They just never get around to doing the actual thing that would help them fulfill their dream.

Have you ever been really focused on something and yet didn't get anywhere with it? At the beginning of this book, I pointed out that a lifetime of a motivational diet had left me short in life. I had not grown in the way I had wanted to in either my professional or personal life. The discussion in this chapter about acting, or rather acting as in taking action, is instructive but not quite complete. The need for focus is important when deciding what you will do about your dreams, but even focus alone won't cut it. You will need to align your actions to your focus. Alignment isn't just for the wheels on your car, it's key to achieving what you want out of life.

I was very focused on self-help and motivation, yet, what I actually did wasn't aligned to that focus. For years I would decorate my office in modern motivation—you know, the inspirational sayings, pictures of the dream house, nice car, whatever. Intense focus without intentional actions that are meant to achieve your desired outcomes is really just an obsession. The results are lots of activity with little to show for it—except perhaps a very inspiring workspace. It is important to have the right kind of focus.

What would you say if I asked you, "What is the difference between the light that comes from a flashlight and a laser?" Most people will say that a laser is more focused than a flashlight. This, however, is not totally correct.

Both the light from a laser and a flashlight are made up of light particles (photons). In a laser, the photons are on the same wavelength, aligned with each other and headed in the same direction with the same level of energy. Think of a laser beam like a column of soldiers marching in a parade in perfect lockstep. Not only that, but they are all in the same color of uniform.

The photons from a flashlight, however, are not aligned. The photons in a beam of light from a flashlight are barely even focused. Think of a big mob of hippies in rainbow tie-dyed shirts, moving more or less in the same direction. The light from a flashlight has all the colors of the rainbow mixed in it because the photons are all at a different energy levels.

The alignment of light particles makes all the difference between lasers and flashlights, and what can be accomplished with each one. Lasers can do amazing things. The beam of light that comes out of a laser can cut through steel, play music in a CD player, ring up your groceries at the checkout counter, repair the cornea in a human eye, or shoot down incoming intercontinental ballistic missiles—you know, the Star Wars defense initiative. Although very useful, a flashlight can simply help you see better in the dark. Yes, sometimes that is exactly what you need, some illumination in your life. If you want to get things accomplished once you can see where you are going, though, you will need to get your actions aligned to that vision.

If you want something to show for your dreams, performance is necessary. All the world is a stage, and you are a player, as the Bard penned. Life, however, more often than not, resembles improv theater as opposed to a stage production. When you are on the stage in improv theater, you never really know what is coming your way–but you have the tools to handle it and make it entertaining. You learn the skills needed to take random circumstances and remarks, and weave a funny performance out of them. Even in improv, your acting is intentional. It needs to be the same for your dreams as well. And, if you dream of becoming a famous actor, well who will complain if you end up making it happen? Make whatever your dream is happen with intentional acting.

It's better than trying to live those dreams vicariously through your kids. Let them live their own dreams–you have yours to get going on. Who knows, they might actually pay attention more to what you do than what you have been trying to tell them all these years. Give them something to pay attention to–it will be one of the best gifts they will ever receive. If you don't have kids or never intend to, it doesn't matter. Your actions will always be one of the best gifts you can give someone. As we will explore later, it's not all about you anyway–as disappointing as you may find that. Your dreams may be yours, but what happens as a result of achieving them will be something that benefits those who you love and care about.

✿ EXPERIENCE A GROWTH SPURT ✿

*Get up and start performing if you want
something to show for your dreams.*

The Yellow Brick Road
Never Was Easy Street

There are potholes in the road to success, not to mention idiot drivers who are on their cellphones, but that doesn't mean you're on the wrong road.

You may find dreaming to be a great escape from the unpleasant realities of your life without all the complications of alcohol and drugs. Dreaming of a better job and life can be intoxicating at times—might even beat a runners high. My dreams are often full of fantasy and always void of unpleasant realities. Dreaming is fun, but reality kind of gets in the way. Apparently, just about everything that is really cool, great, and awesome to obtain—your dreams being on top of the list—has its opposition and challenges.

I grew up in Portland, Oregon, where blackberry bushes grew like weeds. You can find them growing along roadways, in fields, in ditches, on the edges of forests, just about everywhere. Because there's a lot of rain and moisture, the blackberries that grow on these bushes are plump and sweet—unlike those I have had from drier regions of this country. As a kid, my friends and I would often go pick and eat them. They were so sweet and juicy—just like candy.

As good as these Oregon blackberries are, however, there is a hazard to picking them. Blackberry bushes are thorny, very thorny. It seems that no matter how hard you try to avoid getting scratched, pricked, and even cut, it still happens. We didn't care though–tourniquets and band-aids could take care of whatever injuries we sustained. The scratches and cuts were just a part of getting to those berries. If you wanted the berries, you had to deal with the thorns–and we wanted those berries much more than we wanted to avoid injury.

Your dreams have thorns. Thorns can be mistakes you will make, failed attempts, rejection, time you will waste or that will pass where nothing happens in spite of your best efforts, not doing things right in the first place, not knowing how to do something, discouragement, lack of belief or faith in your abilities, others not coming through for you on promises or things they said they would do, others discouraging you overtly or covertly, other conflicting commitments and obligations, lack of money, the demands of other priorities for your time and energy, and so on and so on and so on.

The question isn't will there be thorns, because there will be. If your dream is as desirable as those blackberries were to us kids, then the "thorns" will be incidental and simply what you must get through to obtain your dream. You will gladly bleed–if you must– for what you want.

Remember the 1939 movie *The Wizard of Oz?* Maybe you even read the book, *The Wonderful Wizard of Oz.* For over one hundred years now, scholars, historians, and economists, have all taken a whack at attempting to explain the allegories behind the story–academics really need a life sometimes–I say that out of jealously. It would be great to make a living reading children's stories by dead authors and writing papers that most adults can't even understand about what those now deceased authors really meant.

Some scholars think the story was actually a political metaphor, with the characters like the cowardly lion representing a real politician of that time—big stretch there. We just never stop hating our politicians, do we? One theory that has been advanced is that L. Frank Baum's story was an allegory of the Populist movement and monetary policy as represented by the gold brick road and Dorothy's silver shoes. In the movie version, Dorothy's shoes became the now famous ruby red color in order to take advantage of the new color film technology. Red pops. The gold brick road just became the yellow brick road.

In the story, Dorothy wants to get back home to Kansas. The Scarecrow wants a brain. The Tin Man wants a heart and the Cowardly Lion wants courage. Everyone they meet tells them they need to see the Wonderful Wizard of Oz who will be able to give them what they seek. On their way to the Emerald City—apparently not Seattle—they run into a number of obstacles. They must deal with kalidahs (beasts with the body of a bear and head of tiger) and deadly poppies.

Once they get to the Emerald City and are allowed to see the Wizard, he tells them that before he will help them, they must kill the Wicked Witch of the West and bring back her broomstick. Murder for hire in a children's book—maybe Baum did have a political agenda or some more nefarious message to corrupt the youth of the day when he wrote the story. You never know about those children's stories—maybe there is an academic paper in that.

The Wizard tells them that if they are successful at the task of getting the broomstick, he will give each of them what they have come for. What I don't understand is why they agree to this. "Sure, we will go kill a witch for you." Apparently killing witches is okay in Oz—and most fairy tales for that matter, come to think of it. Perhaps Dorothy and her friends should have thought about it a little more, but apparently they didn't. After all, what better way to get a heart, intelligence, courage or find your way home than by killing a witch and taking her broomstick? But they are desperate to get these things.

So off they go and face more challenges–killer bees, crows that want to peck their eyes out, ravenous wolves, and Winkie soldiers. Once again, they manage to overcome these additional obstacles. Frustrated by our heroes' success, the Wicked Witch calls in the flying monkeys to capture Dorothy and her dog Toto.

Skipping ahead in the story, the Wicked Witch ends up with a bucket of water in the face and melts–killing her. With the witch's demise, it turns out everyone is happy. The Winkie soldiers are free of the witch's tyranny, the flying monkeys are free from a spell they were under, and Dorothy gets the broomstick. It seems a lot of people wanted the witch offed and were quite happy to see her go where the goblins go–below, below, below.

So when the foursome get back to the Emerald City with the broomstick, the Wizard gives them what they each wanted, right? No. He doesn't. He actually tries to turn them away. Toto, however, ends up exposing the Wizard. It turns out he is just a guy from Omaha who knew how to put on a good show. He got people, or rather the various denizens of Oz, to believe he had all the answers when really he didn't.

When Dorothy and her companions discover the truth about the wizard, he lets them in on a secret; they had what they needed all along to achieve their dreams. The Wizard couldn't give them what they sought, because he didn't have it to give. They had to discover that they were able to overcome whatever obstacles stood in their way. They hadn't lacked the means of overcoming their challenges, only confidence in themselves that they could. Regardless of the political metaphors that might lurk within the story, one message was pretty clear–have confidence in yourself because you have what it takes to overcome whatever obstacles stand in the way of your dreams.

Dorothy had the means to get back home right at her feet, or rather on her feet–those snazzy shoes of hers. You can't go wrong with a good pair of shoes. The Lion, the Scarecrow, and the Tin Man already had what they sought: courage, intelligence, and a heart. All the Wizard could give them was insight into their own abilities. Like Dorothy and her friends, we often lack confidence in our own abilities to obtain our dreams, often thinking we lack what we need to achieve them. We can lack confidence as individuals and organizations can also lack confidence in their own abilities to do what they must to thrive and prosper, so they call in experts.

When I was the Director of Human Resources for the company referred to in Chapter 2, we found ourselves facing some significant challenges. It was a real estate asset and development company which had been around for over eighty years. Times were a-changing, however, and we headed into one of the most severe financial downturns to hit our economy. Not only that, but there were rumblings about a corporate reorganization from our parent holding company–which as you will recall, eventually did end up with a merger taking place. Prior to the merger though, we reasoned we had better engage a consulting firm. We wanted them to tell us how we could make our company competitive for the coming challenges we were facing.

It just so happened that the consulting group we hired had written a book called *The Oz Principle*. This consulting group was just as cunning as the Wizard of Oz, although they were more up front with us about the whole process. No hiding behind a curtain, no sending us on quests to retrieve broomsticks and kill witches. They were more into using poster boards and markers to get the job done. They put all the responsibility for finding the answers on us and told us we had to do all the work, and then pay them. They called it "facilitating".

As any human resources person can tell you, dealing with people is a mixed blessing. There were times I thought it would have been easier to fire everyone and hire Oompa Loompas–like Willy Wonka did at his chocolate factory. Never mind whatever labor and immigration laws he might have broken. Oompa Loompas worked for chocolate and sang while they worked. Tell me that's not a good work environment with happy and engaged employees. We didn't have Oompa Loompas though, we had people. So we had to work with them and most of the time–if ever–they did not make up songs and sing while they worked, let alone buy into the idea that chocolate was an acceptable form of compensation.

Like Dorothy and her friends, we found that we had the answers we had been looking for all along within our own organization, with the very people I would have traded for Oompa Loompas some days. We gained confidence in ourselves and in our ability to do what had to be done–that *we* could do it. The consultants, like the Wizard, helped us see what we had and made it clear they didn't have it to give to us. They still took our money.

A big obstacle for me was always my age–it's never been right. First I thought I was too young and then I became too old, and somehow in all that time I missed that "right" age. If you believe much of the media, if you haven't "made it" by time you are out of your twenties, well, maybe the best you can do is be made into Soylent Green. It is a hungry world after all, especially with all those young ambitious types. It was Facebook founder Mark Zuckerberg, who at twenty-two years old proclaimed that, "Young people are just smarter." Maybe it was just Zuckerberg who was smarter. Look how rich he became.

Mr. Zuckerberg is a little older and wiser these days. If he lived in the dystopian future society of the movie *Logan's Run,* he would have had to report to Carrousel–or started running. Even so, don't you ever feel like maybe your best days are behind you? I have felt like that, and some days still do. Fortunately, I, too, have become not just older, but also wiser. Thankfully, I don't live in a dystopian world (although some might say it's a dysfunctional world) and I don't have to report to Carrousel or be hunted down for not showing up. In fact, I am a member of a protected class because of my age thanks to Title VII of the Civil Rights Act. Forty is the new thirty, but now we protect our "old" folks, at least from discrimination in the workplace.

Sometimes people quit trying or caring after years of not living their dreams and conclude it's too late to even try. Sure, their heart keeps beating and their lungs continue to respire, but engaged thinking stops and they exist from day to day on their autonomic nervous system– the undead that continue to walk–zombies. Their flesh may not be rotting but they aren't really living either. And like a zombie, they stumble through life with no purpose. At least a zombie has a purpose–eat the brains of living people. And they pursue that purpose relentlessly. There are lessons to be learned from zombies.

Someone once asked me, "Why stumble over what is behind you?" To which I say, yes, why do that, especially if it is the years you have already lived that you are tripping over? You can't go back in time. Time machines haven't been invented yet. I am given to understand, however, that we will be getting time machines about the same time flying cars come along–which I will park in the garage of my dream house. Until then, you and I are stuck in the present, and always will be. Yet, our present is not static.

Although nothing can be done about the past–just don't tell a history revisionist that–your present may be full of valuable resources acquired over time. It may also have provided you with present day resources in terms of relationships nurtured in your private and professional lives. You may even have a measure of financial resources you didn't have when you were younger–even if those financial resources aren't what you want them to be–yet.

At some point, I started to realize that just because I was older didn't mean I was dumber. Sure I am less cool, (just ask my kids), but not dumber (on second thought, don't ask my kids anything). I also realized that I had resources now–both financially and socially–that I didn't have when I was younger and full of vim, vigor, and inexperience.

I had been looking way too much at what I thought I had lost in terms of the opportunities and not at what I had actually gained over the years, like respect at the grocery store–I have been called "sir" while checking out my purchases. Besides respect at the grocery store, I had also acquired knowledge and experience. I now had resources in terms of personal attributes and awareness that were far more developed than they had ever been at any point in my life. Perhaps, I had never been better prepared or equipped to achieve my dreams. It was a thought at least, a consideration.

I had also gained skills in the course of my career in terms of dealing with people and knowing how to get things done. I had technical skills. I also had financial and physical assets that I had acquired over time, that could be used to help me achieve my goals. Not that I was rich, but I was certainly much better off than when I was just starting out in life. I had also developed relationships, personal and professional, that might be of value in the pursuit of my dreams. I had experience and maturity–never mind what my wife might think about my maturity.

Maybe your chance for success–whatever that means to you now– has increased over the years if you are willing to start using these tangible and intangible assets in helping you to achieve your dreams. Did you know, for example, that older entrepreneurs, as a group, are actually more successful than younger ones—even if they aren't "smarter" according to some sources?

In spite of what the media may have you believing, it isn't true that only twenty-somethings ever start successful companies. They just start all the cool new tech companies. Actually, across the board, even in tech companies, older experienced men and women are more successful in business. Most successful startups are started and run by those who have a few decades of life experience under their belt.

Vivek Wadhwa, a technology entrepreneur and academic who has conducted some interesting studies regarding age and business success, states that, "The young may have good ideas, but there is no substitute for experience." He points out that people are not born with the management, marketing, and financial skills needed to turn ideas into successful companies. His research showed that in successful engineering and technology companies—successful meaning those with actual revenues—the median age of top executives was 39. The average age of the male founders was 40, and the average age of the female founders was 41—the time in life when the Federal Government has put them in a protected class for being old—and yet they are just hitting their stride.

Dane Stangler, Vice President of Research & Policy at the Kauffman Foundation, has pointed out that experience, the contacts, the networks, the ability to recruit good management teams, and education obtained, gives this older group of entrepreneurs a great advantage over young people fresh out of school. Think about it. Who has the money to fund these cool young hipster tech startups that have no revenue? It is older, wiser venture capitalists who usually provide older, wiser business advisors to the companies they fund. Even smart young people need guidance, especially when millions of dollars of venture money is involved. Experience counts.

Perhaps you find yourself still clinging to the idea that something different might still be possible for you. Maybe being a rock star is out, but do you really want to sleep on a tour bus or in hotel rooms for weeks on end? Besides, spandex might not look so cool on you these days. Let's also be honest, sometimes the dreams of our youth are not necessarily the dreams we have now, which is quite okay. Dreams aren't static, nor do they have to die, they can grow up.

I get that with all the experience you gained, you also gained obligations. But ask yourself, when is it going to be the best time to go after your dream? When you are finished with college? After you get the right job? After you buy a house? When the kids move out of the house? When the house is paid off? When you retire? When you downsize? When you do what? There will always be a lot of very, very good reasons not to do it now. It was the case when you were younger, and it will be the case up to the day you die an old bitter man or woman full of resentment and regret for having always put off your dreams.

As I thought about my own situation, I realized how true this was. I still had kids at home, a mortgage to pay, retirement savings to think about, family, church and community obligations to attend to, and aging parents who needed help. There have been and always will be many very good reasons why you should wait to get serious about pursuing your dreams. The idea that there will be a better time to work on your dreams is based on the false idea that at some point the obstacles will not exist–sometime in that wonderful future that never comes. Reality will always be in the way.

Age does bring experience and, hopefully, wisdom, although wisdom isn't guaranteed. I will assume though that you, regardless of how old you are, as a result of living, have gained a little wisdom along the way. A little wisdom and experience are a powerful combination. So right off the bat you should realize that if you decide to go for your dreams, you already have some very important attributes that will help you obtain those dreams.

So maybe you aren't as young as you used to be. You never are, and you won't be tomorrow, either, or anytime in the future—even if you are still in your twenties. No matter what age you are, take advantage of what experience has given you thus far to navigate the obstacles that come with your dreams.

The growth you need to achieve your dreams is going to take a commitment and concerted effort. There will come a time as you pursue your dream that you will come up against obstacles—pretty much guaranteed. If you decide to make a commitment to pursue your dreams, you may experience discomfort and even pain as you face these obstacles. The good news is, however, that it won't be ordinary discomfort or pain, it will be growing pains. It is pain with a purpose.

Have you ever been serious about weight training and building muscles? If you have you know what pain that has a purpose is all about. It's where the phrase, "no pain no gain," comes from. Of course we also get the phrase "dumbbell" from weight training. There is truth in the phrase, "no pain no gain." To build muscles, you must break it down and let it repair itself. There is pain in this process but you end up looking like a Greek god. The reward for doing what it takes is worth the pain and effort—if you want your dream enough. It is obvious in my case that looking like a Greek god isn't my dream. I'd rather eat ice cream—so I run and settle for "not overweight."

I am not going to say that pain is fun—unless you are the type who likes pain—but for all the kinds of pain you experience in life, growing pains at least get you to a much better place. If you want to achieve your dreams, you will have to grow. As you overcome, get through, get past, or around the obstacles to your dreams, be prepared for some discomfort or pain—and deal with it.

When I was a kid, I knew I was going to get cut and scraped reaching into those thorny blackberry bushes, but I also knew how good those blackberries were going to be—and they were. If you want to achieve your dreams, whatever they are, have the courage to face and deal with the thorns. Just be glad no one is asking you to go fetch broomsticks from a witch.

⚙ EXPERIENCE A GROWTH SPURT ⚙

Get used to the pain of growing so that you can enjoy the pleasures of success.

When You Get There,
Say "Hello" To The Mouse For Me

More often than not, the question isn't if you have the ability to do it, but rather if you will choose to do it.

There comes a point in your life when you must make a choice, at least if you expect to get anywhere with your high hopes and big dreams—or even your little ones for that matter. You will need to choose a direction and make a commitment to follow it. Commitment to direction opens doors of opportunity. Like focus (remember lasers versus flashlights?), there is difference between a decision and a committed decision. Commitment means action and action takes you places.

The real growth you will experience comes after the decision to do something is made and you have begun to act on your commitment—which begs the question, "What are you committed to doing?" When you answer that question, your dreams are well on their way to becoming realities. Until you make that commitment, it's all nice and good but not real yet. Committing to action will give you one of the most important attributes you need to grow—courage.

Often there is a point in your life when you have an opportunity to make a choice between taking a new path in life or reaffirming your commitment to the one you are already on. The choice you make depends on what you want and whether or not your current direction will take you there. Sometimes, there are conflicting values involved maybe comfort in the familiar versus discomfort in the unknown. Sometimes, it means changing values or beliefs. Your actions, after all, stem from what you value and believe. It you want to go in a different direction, one that will lead to your dream, you may need to change a few things.

I am not suggesting you change values and beliefs just to get what you want. I am also not saying to give up values such as compassion, charity, morality, friendship, family or good food–unless good food is getting in the way of your dream to lose weight. In that case, adopt the value of eating good healthy food in moderation. I adopted the value of exercise so I could continue to eat large amounts of ice cream. Okay, I had to throw in a little moderation as well–yeah, right. Whatever your dream is, there will be a time when you must make a committed decision to what you will do to achieve it. This can be a significant turning point in your life, a crossroads.

For the last ten years I have lived at the Crossroads of the West–Salt Lake City. Not long ago I found myself at the Crossroads of the World–Disney Hollywood Studios in Orlando. As you enter the park on Hollywood Boulevard, there is a small souvenir shop with a tower built on top of it. At the top of the tower is a large globe and standing on that globe is Mickey Mouse. At the base of the tower are the words, in blue neon lights, "Crossroads of the World." The iconic tower is modeled after the original one located at the Crossroads of the World outdoor mall (now business offices) on Sunset Boulevard in Los Angeles. The original, however, doesn't have Mickey on it waving to you.

As I looked at this sign, I began to think about crossroads, in a metaphorical way. Crossroads are a place where life-changing decisions are made—a place of choices and commitments. My vision of the crossroads was always a place where two lonely country roads intersect at a place where there is nothing around for miles but empty countryside. The air is still and hot, the humidity high, like a midsummer day in the Deep South. If you have ever lived in the south, and I have, you know what those hot, humid summer days can feel like—oppressive.

Just off to one side of the intersection of those two lonely roads is a very large and ancient oak tree. Underneath this ancient oak, out of the sunlight and in the shade, leaning with his back against the trunk, is the devil, Satan. He is sometimes called "the black man" in literature. I always envision him being tall, thin and dressed in a dark suit—like an undertaker from the 1800s. He is there waiting for you, ready to make some Faustian deal for your soul. All you have to do is sign his contract with your blood. No big deal, your soul for fame and fortune.

I am not one to attribute nefarious intentions to Mickey Mouse, although I have felt at times like I have sold my soul to Disney with all the money I've spent at Disney theme parks—and Mickey is an all-black mouse. Really though, when you think about it, if I had sold my soul to Disney, I would be rich and famous, not the mouse—he would just have my soul. Besides, some might argue I already sold my soul when I went to law school. I know, you aren't supposed to think too deeply at Disney theme parks. It kills the magic.

Crossroads are situations where critical choices are made that shape your life—a direction is chosen. While on a Disney cruise with my family in the Carribbean, I learned something about the importance of knowing where you are going and making the right choice in direction. On one of the nights we watched a stage production with a very clear message: all it takes to achieve your dreams is belief and pixie dust. I agree it takes belief to achieve your dreams but making a commitment to a direction you will take works a lot better than pixie dust. Besides, where are you going to get pixie dust? They were kind of vague about that. If they had it, they would have been selling it in the gift shop–duty free.

When you lack a good sense of direction, literally or metaphorically, you can end up quite lost. One of the ports of call on that cruise was St. Maarten. The island is divided between two countries, The Netherlands and France. The cruise ships dock in the Dutch city of Philipsburg. Once you disembark from the ship, you are free to travel the entire island. It was here that we (and a couple of other families that had joined us on the cruise) decided to rent scooters and tour the island as a group. We ended up hanging out at Friar's Beach on the French side of the Island.

After spending an afternoon at Friar's Beach, we decided we would all visit Fort Saint-Louis and then head back to the ship. When we came to the city of Marigot, somehow our entire party became separated. I know how it happened for me. I went the wrong way down a one-way street with my twelve-year-old son on the back of my scooter. At that point, we had become completely lost from the rest of the group. I figured, no problem, just keep following the main road as it circled around the entire island. How hard could that be? If you will recall, my sense of direction isn't always really great–the whole right/left, east/west thing.

With my keen sense of direction, my son and I proceeded to head into the interior of the island until I figured out that I was moving further and further from the ocean. The road we wanted circled the island close to the sea. When you lack a sense of direction, you can really end up in places you don't want to be. Thank goodness, the people were friendly and helpful and I at least knew where I wanted to get to–back to the ship in Philipsburg on the Dutch side of the island. Even so, it wasn't so easy. At one point, I found myself at a crossroads, literally, and had to make my best guess at which direction to go. Thankfully I got it right, because by this time the sun was beginning to set. I was starting to wonder what I would do if our ship sailed without us. I was getting pretty nervous about our situation. It was dusk when we eventually made it back to where we had rented our scooters that morning. Thankfully we made it back to the ship before it set sail.

That evening, safe and sound back on the ship, and reunited with my family, we all laughed at the little adventure. My wife and our eight-year-old son had actually made it to the fort we had all intended to visit until the big separation happened. She is much better at direction. She would never go on the television show, *The Amazing Race,* with me–she is wise in this regard. When you don't have a sense of direction, it's really hard to get where you want to go.

A commitment to a destination can help give you direction. You may have to stop and ask for help, more than once or twice. You may not always be sure which way is the right way, but if you know where you want to go, you have a much better chance of getting there. Commit to a destination to your dreams and you have a much better chance to achieve them.

Dian Thomas wrote a New York Times bestselling book called *Roughing It Easy,* a book full of clever ideas for cooking in the great outdoors. The book led to an appearance on *The Tonight Show* with Johnny Carson, which launched her into a career in television. She went on to work eight years as a regular on NBC's *Today Show* and then for six years on ABC's *Home Show.* Dian appeared several times on ABC's *Good Morning America* as well as numerous other national and local television programs. She continues to be a professional speaker, spokeswomen, author, columnist, and television personality. We met quite by chance. I was in New York City for the first time, the same trip where I met New York Jeff. I met some very cool people on that trip.

One evening I had planned to explore Central Park. Unfortunately– or so I thought at the time–my plans were rained out. As I stood in the rain, I decided I would find a friendly person at the local meetinghouse of the church I belong to, which happened to be near, and ask them for some suggestions. I wasn't disappointed because this was where I met Dian, who was also in New York on business. We began talking and learned that we were actually neighbors back home in Salt Lake City. After some initial pleasantries and a few suggestions of what I might explore the rest of the evening, I was off to the Metropolitan Museum of Art. I LOVED the Met. It turned out to be my favorite part of that trip. My right brain proclivities had a party there.

When I returned home I decided to get in touch with Dian and ask her about her career. For several years I had been writing magazine articles. I enjoyed doing it and I enjoyed the side income. Writing those articles had paid for my family's Disney cruise. I had this vague desire to do something "more" with my writing. I wasn't really sure what "more" was. I decided I would contact Dian and ask her about her career path and get any advice she might have. I needed some direction.

When we met I showed her my portfolio of magazine articles and when I was done, she said to me, "Jeff, writing is only about 20% of what you need to be doing." You need to understand the entire spectrum of communications and publicity." She then began to explain to me about professional speaking, and an organization called NSA. Now you might be thinking that the NSA is the National Security Agency–the secretive intelligence agency that listens to all the electronic communications that go on in the world. No, the NSA that Dian was referring to wasn't the organization that listens. It was the organization that speaks–the National Speakers Association.

After attending my third meeting, without having joined, the president of the chapter pulled me aside to ask me when I was going to join. I told him I wasn't sure I wanted to but I liked what I was learning. I told him that I didn't know if it was something I wanted to do, become a professional speaker. He then shot back at me, "Jeff, you won't know that answer until you make a commitment and do something about it–and besides I will give you a great membership discount if you commit to join now." So I joined. Basically, I had been given a direction by being introduced to NSA, but I needed to make a commitment to that direction.

I still didn't make that commitment right off and (big surprise) it led me nowhere. For a long time I went to the meetings and people were always asking me, "What do you speak on?" My reply was, "I have no message to give and no audience to give it to–so it works out pretty well."

It was a great example of what I have referred to earlier in regards to doing stuff but without any alignment of purpose–riding ponies when it's the bull you need to be jumping on. Every time I went to a meeting, I felt like I was in the right place doing the right thing. I was hearing incredible stories from incredible people doing incredible things. These people were gregarious extroverts, fun to be around. I on the other hand tended to be a bit introverted, maybe a little insecure and reserved–dull, boring and lacking in enthusiasm. Where was New York Jeff? He was waiting for a commitment to a direction.

I look back on that trip to New York where I met Dian and realize I had come to a crossroads. I had to decide if I was going to continue to be a bit introverted, a little insecure and reserved, or start being New

York Jeff. It was time to change some beliefs about myself. I had to give up the comfort of being an introvert. Not that I became extroverted, but I had to learn when to be one–to act like one–to accomplish my dreams. Riding the bull meant facing fears and discomfort. I had to become a situational extrovert. I need to be willing to exert myself when needed rather than stepping back, which was the more comfortable thing for me to do. My commitment to my dream of doing "more" with my writing required it.

Ask yourself what you need to commit to doing if you want to see your dreams come true. What must you do, so you can be what you need to be, so that you can do what you want to do? I don't know what that is for you, but I know where you can find out–that ever present and at times crazy inner voice you have. It is quite willing to chime in. So trust it and decide to make a commitment or two. You won't have to sell your soul and chances are good you will even find it as you pursue your dreams. No blood contracts required, just a willingness to decide and commit to the very thing you have wanted to do anyway.

✪ EXPERIENCE A GROWTH SPURT ✪

Don't just decide, make a commitment.

Yes, People Are Going to Laugh at You

At some point, you will have to let others know what your dreams are, and that can be one of the most courageous things you will do, because they may not get it.

Ever meet someone who is just physically striking? Anne was that way. Gay or straight, man or woman, Anne often got a second look from people who saw her. Anne was a former model, tall and graceful with black hair, and green eyes. She was the type of person you might be jealous of, or at least self-conscious around because she was so beautiful. Yet she was absolutely warm and accepting towards all she met. Our paths crossed when she was an instructor in a career course I took.

Anne told us a story about how others will sometimes react to our dreams when we share them. It was a cautionary story so we would be prepared when this sort of thing happened to us as we chased our dreams. She taught us to beware of Friday night drunks, and they can be found on any night of the week.

Years ago, she and a group of friends would get together at

a particular bar on Friday nights for good times and socializing. One of the group members was an artist who liked to draw funny pictures and cartoons. One night this artist friend brought in some pictures he had drawn and showed them to the group. The reception he received was less than kind. Anne and her friends laughed at his art and laughed at his dreams. As she put it, they were both drunk and rude.

The artist was Will Vinton, and fortunately he didn't let that night's reception stop him from pursuing his dreams. Vinton went on to become the creator of the animation technique called Claymation®, which uses stop motion cinematography and clay figures. He turned his animation techniques into a commercial success and created many award winning films and commercials. One of Vinton's first films, a short piece called *Closed Mondays,* won an Academy Award. The work he would do for television went on to win Emmys.

It was his studio that created the famous singing and dancing "California Raisins" commercial where a group of Claymation® raisins sang *"I Heard It Through the Grapevine."* Other notable works of Vinton's include the television show *The PJs,* starring Eddy Murphy. His studios also created the Noid character that appeared in a series of Domino Pizza advertisements. This was the artist that Anne and her friends laughed at that Friday night in the bar.

It seems that no matter what your dream is, you will run up against critics, naysayers, mockers, a "peanut gallery" full of hecklers, skeptics, and Friday night drunks. They might even be family or friends—as I would find out for myself. Anne and her friends were a bunch of Friday night drunks. As you pursue your dreams, there will be Friday night drunks, but you can't let them stop you.

This lesson really came home for me the night I took part in the fire walk. When the event was over, I headed directly to a party my wife and I had been invited to attend. My wife was already there, having gone to the party ahead of me while I played in the fire. When I arrived at the party, I smelled like a campfire. I am surprised no one commented to me about it. I really did stink. In hindsight I should have taken a shower and changed clothes before I went to the party. Maybe it explained the reception I received.

I was totally excited about what I had just experienced and wanted to share my excitement with everyone at the party, who, for the most part, I knew and were my friends. I was expecting them to get as excited as I was. I was completely surprised by their response. They didn't get excited. Rather, they were very skeptical of the whole experience and made comments like, "There has to be some kind of scientific explanation," or "You're crazy for having done that," and "You couldn't get me to do something so foolish." I was being called a liar and a fool. These people weren't even drunk. They were totally missing the point. "Idiots," I wanted to call them. I felt hurt. They weren't getting it and I was feeling attacked.

I wasn't suggesting we all go walk on broken glass and through an open fire pit–although by the reception I was getting, it might have done them some good. Let's see who gets burned now–ha, ha, ha. Actually, I really wanted them to see what was possible, how the seemingly impossible could be possible. I tried to tell them how it felt to be terrified and yet find out that it was possible to do things one never had considered doing before. I wanted them to be as excited as I was. Just think what else might be possible given what I had just done! But they didn't get it.

My own excitement began to fade as I was faced with their negative reception. It had only been a few hours and already I was facing "Friday night drunks" who happened to be stone cold sober. They weren't idiots. I was the idiot. I began to let them tell me how I should feel and think instead of holding on to the belief in myself that

I had experienced–the belief that had allowed me to do things I never thought I would or could do.

Belief in yourself isn't just about you. Having a strong belief in oneself can be one of the most unselfish things you can do, especially when others, like a family, rely on you. When you are confident, you radiate something that others feel and want to be a part of. You take away their fears and insecurities. Your confidence allows them to be who they need to be. This is extremely important for those who are closest to you and whom you care about the most. They need your confidence. And you need to give it to them.

Willamette University, where I earned my law degree, has the motto, "Non nobis solum nati sumus–Not unto ourselves alone are we born." The law school had its own motto, "Omnia enim propter nosmet ipsos–All things for ourselves." Okay, I am only kidding about the law school motto. We didn't have a separate one. We just went with the University's motto.

If you have a significant other, family, or friends that support you in your madness, you are blessed. My wife has been a great support to me. This doesn't, however, mean she supports me in everything I dream up–do you think she's crazy? No, that's my role. She has much better judgment. She has, however, given me more support at times than I deserved. For that reason, I felt that I needed to give her something. She needed me to be confident–something I wasn't too good at. Years of hiding one's true self can really wear you down–of that I am confident. One day I decided I wanted to show her, even if only symbolically and with the hope it would eventually lead to actual results, that I was committed to becoming confident.

You might be thinking that I am about to tell you some really big deal thing I did to show my commitment. You are expecting too much from a man who loves watching *Project Runway*. No, it wasn't a grand gesture. I believe that sincere should outweigh splendor—not that splendor and spectacular don't have their place. It is often the small and simple things we do with true sincerity, however, that have more meaning. I was quite sincere, if not a little crazy. I think my wife just thought I was crazy.

I really like plaid shirts. My wife doesn't—to a very high degree. Maybe it's just when I wear plaid she doesn't like them. Apparently, when I wear them they remind her of two things she doesn't want to be reminded of in a husband. One is her father—whom she loves but doesn't want to be married to. The other is the passive side of my personality—which has been a source of great frustration to her at times—okay, lots of times. She felt that plaid did not exude confidence.

Being the loving and devoted husband that I am, and wanting to support her in her aspirations, (i.e., being married to a spouse who doesn't wear plaid), I took the bold action of one day throwing out all the plaid shirts I owned. I gathered up every plaid shirt in my closet and donated them to the thrift shop. As much as she dislikes me wearing plaid, she thought this was a bit crazy on my part.

Maybe she would have felt differently about me wearing plaids if I also wore a kilt. Well, yes, of course she would feel differently about me if I wore a kilt, but that isn't necessarily the way I wanted her to feel differently about me. You have to be very confident to wear a kilt. Scots are among the most confident people I know. Well, the one Scot I know is very confident. Among other things, he was involved in a New York fashion charity event, *Dressed to Kilt*. They actually walk down a runway, in front of people, in kilts. That is confidence. In my native northwest, very manly men, like lumberjacks, wear plaid shirts—and carry big chain saws. I am not a lumberjack or a Scot, so I really had no good argument when it came to why I should persist in wearing plaid shirts.

For me, this defining day of wardrobe demarcation represented not only a change in my sense of fashion—and a loss of over half the shirts I owned—but a change in my consciousness. I decided I could, and I would, believe in myself, and in my dreams. Not just for myself, but for someone I cared about more than myself. It was this bold act of plaid purging that represented one of my mental turning points, I realized that believing in oneself is not a selfish act, because nothing says "I love you" like confidence—and maybe chocolate.

Honestly, I still miss the plaid shirts and it is a lot harder to buy casual dress shirts. Just try flipping through a men's clothing catalog like Eddie Bauer or going shopping at Costco to find a casual men's shirt that isn't plaid. I would have been better off having been a confident individual in the first place. I would still be able to wear plaid and not have such a hard time shopping for shirts these days. I have, however, stuck confidently to wearing at least one type of plaid shirt, madras plaid. I personally really like the bright lively mix of colors in a madras plaid shirt. They radiate confidence, if you ask me. My wife doesn't ask me.

Donating my shirts to charity didn't make me confident. Neither did walking on fire make me brave. But they were outward actions of a changing mental attitude I was experiencing. I was growing. I was still physically short but I was starting to stand, and more importantly, think taller. If I think about it, perhaps I am better off wearing striped shirts anyway, they make me look taller—the vertical stripe patterns that is.

You should not let people who laugh at or mock you stop you from confidently pursuing your dreams. If your best supporters don't like your wardrobe, maybe it's time for a makeover. You don't change because they want you to; you change because you love them as much or more than you love yourself. They aren't the ones who will be laughing at you, because they want to see you be successful. Ignore the Friday night drunks who don't care about you.

✿ EXPERIENCE A GROWTH SPURT ✿

Pursue your dreams not only for yourself,
but because you love someone else even more.

In Short, Think Taller

Had I thought about it,
I could have been taller years ago.

I think I would have been taller a long time ago if I had only thought about it. You don't need a chair to stand taller–maybe to reach the top shelf in the closet–but not to stand taller in your life. Speaking of closets, is it time to come out of yours? Whatever it might be? Is it time to let others know who you really are, time to accept it yourself?

I don't expect you to change your whole life because you read this book–just change something. Something that matters, something that will make a difference, that will get you closer, even if only a little closer, to your dreams. Don't be the same, even if no one notices. Do it because you care enough to change something in your life that you should have changed a long time ago.

Now if you want to have fun, change something big and see how those around you react–but that may take more courage than you have right now. That's okay, because if you are serious and determined to be who you are, not who others think you are supposed to be, or who you have been afraid to be, then that will come–and you will welcome it.

It does "take courage to grow up and be who you are," as E.E. Cummings penned. Courage is what you do. It's not always what you feel when facing your fears—unless you are high and out of your mind on chemical substances—which is not recommended. For most of us, courage is the aftermath of having acted on our beliefs in the face of our fears. Courage is an action and happiness is its by product—it's best not to confuse the two.

Belief can change not only what you are willing to do, but it can change what you are able to do. Belief is the best thing I know for motivating you to action, including things like walking over fires and karate chopping boards in half. It is also what you will need to achieve your dreams—the belief you can do it.

It is true that better thinking equals better results in your personal and professional life. Practice it if need be, because what you think matters and what you do counts. It's not just what you think; it's also how you think that matters. A good framework will help with that, so learn one and use it.

Remember that persistence does work, but it isn't always easy. Perhaps like Henry Ford mentioned about thinking being such hard work, it's the same with persistence, and hence why so few keep at it. Do not be one of those people. Find a reason to keep going, even if it's so you can eat another bowl of ice cream—there are worse reasons. Do it because, in doing, are things done. Yes, performance requires acting. It also requires that you decide to act. Few decisions are as important as the ones made about your commitments.

When faced with the inevitable obstacles that will present themselves as you follow the yellow brick road to your dreams, remember you have the solutions you need already within you. You are neither too young nor too old. It gets back to having confidence in yourself. Listen with trust and confidence to the voice in your head and ignore the inner critic. Your inner voice has your best interest at heart, and is a lot easier to live with when obeyed. You never know where it will lead and the fun that is in store for you. It just might introduce you to yourself and you will find you have a new best friend.

Everyone loves success, or so they say. In reality, they admire it but often find it uncomfortable when someone they know is experiencing it. Don't let that discourage you from chasing your dreams and making them happen. There are those who love you because you are finding success and making your dreams come true. These are the people who will wonder about you–in a very good way. They will wonder where you have been hiding all this time. They will love you for who you are, what you have become, and who you are becoming. You don't have to tell them you have been hiding in a closet waiting for a Wizard to tell you to go fetch a broomstick. Just throw out your plaid shirts and they will get the picture.

I wish you all that is good and right in your journey to achieving your dreams. Run free, run fast, but by all means, run. You may have thought you were going to be taller, but that was then. Start growing today and see what heights you end up reaching now. In the end, don't sell yourself short–have the courage to *be* taller by thinking taller in everything you do.

❀ EXPERIENCE A GROWTH SPURT ❀

Have the courage to think taller because life is short, but you don't have to be.

In Summary

The Tall And Short Of Things

*"Being tall isn't a matter of feet or inches.
It's a matter of courage."*

❂ GROWTH SPURT ❂

To be taller, start thinking taller.

Coming Out of the Right Closet

*"It takes a lot of energy being someone you aren't,
nor are you ever really good at it."*

❂ GROWTH SPURT ❂

***Find the courage to be who you are
and resist the urge to run away.***

3

If You Aren't Good at Being You, Maybe You Should Practice More

"Everyone wants to be an individual. The problem is that very few people want to be one by themselves."

❂ GROWTH SPURT ❂

Stop being normal and start being you.

4

You Can't Poke Out the Mind's Eye or Muzzle the Voice in Your Head

"If you can't trust yourself, it's time you learned how. Otherwise your dreams will remain locked away where no one will be able to get to them, not even you."

❂ GROWTH SPURT ❂

Trust yourself, you're crazy not to.

5

Far Too Many People Are Qualified to be the Village Idiot

"You don't have to be a genius, just be willing to think."

***

❂ GROWTH SPURT ❂

Do the smart thing and learn how to think taller.

6

Four Letter "F" Words–Fear and Fire

"Walking on fire it turns out is easy.
It leaves you wondering what else might be
easier than you had thought it would be."

***

❂ GROWTH SPURT ❂

Face your fears with courage and belief,
even if you must close your eyes to do so.

7

If We Were Meant to Run Naked, We Would be Born That Way

"Run for something, even if it's just so you can eat another bowl of ice cream, but run."

✹ GROWTH SPURT ✹

Keep running to your dreams until you get there. Experience is not required.

8

Performance is Really Just an Act

"Life is usually not scripted so get comfortable with improvisational acting."

✹ GROWTH SPURT ✹

Get up and start performing if you want something to show for your dreams.

9

The Yellow Brick Road Never Was Easy Street

"There are potholes in the road to success, not to mention idiot drivers who are on their cellphones, but that doesn't mean you're on the wrong road."

✹ GROWTH SPURT ✹

Get used to the pain of growing so that you can enjoy the pleasures of success.

10

When You Get There, Say Hello to the Mouse for Me

"More often than not, the question isn't if you have the ability to do it, but rather if you will choose to do it."

✹ GROWTH SPURT ✹

Don't just decide, make a commitment.

11

Yes, People are Going to Laugh at You

"At some point, you will have to let others know what your dreams are, and that can be one of the most courageous things you will do, because they may not get it."

❂ GROWTH SPURT ❂

Pursue your dreams not only for yourself, but because you love someone else even more.

12

In Short, Think Taller

"Had I thought about it, I could have been taller years ago."

❂ GROWTH SPURT ❂

Have the courage to think taller because life is short but you don't have to be.

❂ FOR A FREE DOWNLOADABLE SUMMARY ❂

Go to www.ThinkTaller.com

Acknowledgements

There are a few people I would like to thank. First, there is my wife, Kathy, and our two sons, Adam and Ethan. Without them, not only would my life be quite a bit poorer, but so would this book. Kathy read over countless drafts and rewrites and gave me great suggestions, which have only made this book better. I am sure she would like to see her suggestions for my life implemented with as much care and consideration. As for my sons, they have provided me with great insights as I have watched them grow and mature.

The following people also read through a draft of this book and were kind enough to provide me with many useful observations and suggestions. I am very grateful for their generosity of time, thoughts and even edits. Thank you, Carolyn Campbell, Tom Cantrell, Diane Coles, Jimmy Coray, Richard Doxey, John Evans, Jason Hewlett, Sharee Hughes, Jerry Sanchez, Mark Smith, Sandy Thackery, and Kristy Witt. Your contributions have been invaluable. You all made me look like I could actually write a coherent thought.

Author Biography

Jeff Vanek–January 2015

Jeff understands what it takes for you to grow personally. He knows that growth is rarely a single direction, but it can always make you taller—if you have the courage to reach for your dreams. Jeff started college majoring in communications, ended up graduating with a degree in political science and going off to law school. Ever interested in personal growth, he went back to school and earned a Master's of Science and Technology–midcareer. He figures buying a red sports car might have been more fun in retrospect. Jeff works as a human resources professional helping people grow personally and professionally. Jeff writes articles for magazines on employment, business, and legal issues—with other assorted topics thrown in the mix. He lives at the base of Mt. Olym-pus with his wife, two boys, and dog Lucille Esmeralda McGillicud-dy Ricardo Vanek—who just goes by "Lucy" most days.

Have the Author Speak to Your Organization!

If you found this book entertaining and engaging, you should meet the author! Invite Jeff to speak to your group or organization about finding the courage it takes to grow professionally and personally. Who wouldn't benefit from growing a little taller?

Go to www.ThinkTaller.com